W9-AVZ-815

Cambridge
First Certificate
in English
2

WITHOUT ANSWERS

*Official examination papers
from University of Cambridge
ESOL Examinations*

CAMBRIDGE
UNIVERSITY PRESS

CAMBRIDGE UNIVERSITY PRESS
Cambridge, New York, Melbourne, Madrid, Cape Town, Singapore, São Paulo, Delhi

Cambridge University Press
The Edinburgh Building, Cambridge CB2 8RU, UK

www.cambridge.org
Information on this title: www.cambridge.org/9780521714532

© Cambridge University Press 2008

It is normally necessary for written permission for copying to be obtained *in advance* from a publisher. The candidate answer sheets at the back of this book are designed to be copied and distributed in class. The normal requirements are waived here and it is not necessary to write to Cambridge University Press for permission for an individual teacher to make copies for use within his or her own classroom. Only those pages which carry the wording '© UCLES 2008 Photocopiable ' may be copied.

First published 2008

Printed in the United Kingdom at the University Press, Cambridge

A catalogue record for this book is available from the British Library

ISBN 978-0-521-714532 Student's Book without answers

ISBN 978-0-521-714549 Student's Book with answers

ISBN 978-0-521-714563 Set of 2 Audio CDs

ISBN 978-0-521-714556 Self-study Pack

Contents

Thanks and acknowledgements

The authors and publishers acknowledge the following sources of copyright material and are grateful for the permissions granted. While every effort has been made, it has not always been possible to identify the sources of all the material used, or to trace all copyright holders. If any omissions are brought to our notice, we will be happy to include the appropriate acknowledgements on reprinting.

For the texts on p. 8 and on p. 30, from *Cross my Heart and Hope to Die* by Sheila Radley, 1992. By permission of Constable and Robinson Publishing Ltd; for the text on p. 10, 'The Netball Captain' by Suzie Ellis, from Hello! Online www.hello-online.ru. Copyright © 2003 National Association of Teachers of English; for the article on p. 13, 'Style Merchants' by Jo Foley, *Illustrated London News*, 1998; for the text on p. 32, 'Living in the Valley' by Mike Bell from *Peak and Pennine*, March 1998, © Mike Bell; for the adapted texts by Nina Hathway on p. 35, 'Confident people. What's their secret?' *Woman's Weekly*, February 1997, and on p. 79 from 'Theme Park', *Woman's Weekly*, July 1996, © Copyright IPC Media Ltd, all rights reserved; for the articles from the *Independent* on p. 52, 'The Shell Artist' by Peter Cooke, 27 April 1996, and on p. 74, 'The Film Critic' by Mark Adams, 11 October 1996, © Independent News and Media Limited; for the adapted article on p. 54, 'Chips with Everything' from *Caterer and Hotel Keeper*, 29 January 1998, © The Caterer Group; for the adapted text on p. 63, 'Secret London' by Andrew Duncan, New Holland Publishers (UK Limited); for the adapted article on p. 76, 'Fun at the Dentist's?' by Rose Rouse, *Guardian*, 31 December 1996, © Rose Rouse; for the adapted text on p. 84, 'Downhill Racer' by David Allsopp, *Midweek*, 2–6 February, 1995; for the article on p. 85, 'See you in three years says jogger on lap of the world' by Russell Jenkins, *The Times,* 7 December 1996, © N I Syndication Limited.

For permission to reproduce copyright photographs:

Art Directors & TRIP/C Kapolka for p. 32; The Merrion Hotel, Dublin for p. 54; W Lloyd Jerome for p. 77; Steve Bloom Images/Alamy for p. 90.

Colour section

Alamy/Harold R Stinnette Photo Stock pC6 (bl), Alamy/Mixa Co Ltd pC8 (b), Alamy/Photostock Files pC6 (tr); **Art Directors & Trip** pC1 (b), Art Directors & Trip pC16 (t), Art Directors & Trip/B Gadsby pC13 (b), Art Directors & Trip/Helene Rogers pC6 (tl), Art Directors & Trip/J Stanley pC13 (t); **Corbis**/Jason Hosling/Zefa pC14 (b); **Getty Images**/ Howard Kingsnorth pC9 (t), Getty Images/Alan Klehr pC8 (t), Getty Images/Andy Caulfield pC9 (b), Getty Images/Chris Ladd pC14 (t), Getty Images/Daniel Pangbourne pC14 (c), Getty Images/John Warden pC7 (cr), Getty Images/Stewart Cohen pC5 (tr), Getty/Don Johnston pC7 (tr); **John Birdsall** pC5 (b), pC12 (b), pC15 (bl); **Life File**/Angela Maynard pC15 (br); **Pictures Colour Library** pC4 (all), pC7 (b); **Robert Harding**/Dr Müller pC12 (t); **Sally & Richard Greenhill** pC1 (t), pC16 (b), Sally & Richard Greenhill/Richard Greenhill pC6 (br); **Shout Pictures**/John Callan pC15 (tl); **VCL**/Alistair Berry pC15 (tr).

Artwork by Oxford Designers & Illustrators

Picture research by Alison Prior

Design concept by Peter Ducker

Cover design by David Lawson

The recordings which accompany this book were made at Studio AVP, London.

Introduction

This collection of four complete practice tests comprises papers from the University of Cambridge ESOL Examinations First Certificate in English (FCE) examination; students can practise these tests on their own or with the help of a teacher.

The FCE examination is part of a suite of general English examinations produced by Cambridge ESOL. This suite consists of five examinations that have similar characteristics but are designed for different levels of English language ability. Within the five levels, FCE is at Level B2 in the Council of Europe's *Common European Framework of Reference for Languages: Learning, teaching, assessment*. It has also been accredited by the Qualifications and Curriculum Authority in the UK as a Level 1 ESOL certificate in the National Qualifications Framework. The FCE examination is widely recognised in commerce and industry and in individual university faculties and other educational institutions.

Examination	Council of Europe Framework Level	UK National Qualifications Framework Level
CPE Certificate of Proficiency in English	C2	3
CAE Certificate in Advanced English	C1	2
FCE First Certificate in English	B2	1
PET Preliminary English Test	B1	Entry 3
KET Key English Test	A2	Entry 2

Further information

The information contained in this practice book is designed to be an overview of the exam. For a full description of all of the above exams including information about task types, testing focus and preparation, please see the relevant handbooks which can be obtained from Cambridge ESOL at the address below or from the website at: www.CambridgeESOL.org

University of Cambridge ESOL Examinations
1 Hills Road
Cambridge CB1 2EU
United Kingdom

Telephone: +44 1223 553997
Fax: +44 1223 553621
e-mail: ESOLHelpdesk@ucles.org.uk

The structure of FCE: an overview

The FCE examination consists of five papers.

Paper 1   Reading   1 hour
This paper consists of **three parts**, each containing a text and some questions. Part 3 may contain two or more shorter related texts. There are **30 questions** in total, including multiple-choice, gapped text and multiple-matching questions.

Paper 2   Writing   1 hour 20 minutes
This paper consists of **two parts** which carry equal marks. In Part 1, which is **compulsory**, candidates have to write either a letter or an email of between 120 and 150 words. In Part 2, there are four tasks from which candidates **choose one** to write about. The range of tasks from which questions may be drawn includes an article, an essay, a letter, a report, a review and a short story. The last question is based on the set books. These books remain on the list for two years. Look on the website, or contact the Cambridge ESOL Local Secretary in your area for the up-to-date list of set books. The question on the set books has two options from which candidates **choose one** to write about. In this part, candidates have to write between 120 and 180 words.

Paper 3   Use of English   45 minutes
This paper consists of **four parts** and tests control of English grammar and vocabulary. There are **42 questions** in total. The tasks include gap-filling exercises, word formation and sentence transformation.

Paper 4   Listening   40 minutes (approximately)
This paper consists of **four parts**. Each part contains a recorded text or texts and some questions, including multiple-choice, sentence completion, and multiple-matching. Each text is heard twice. There is a total of **30 questions**.

Paper 5   Speaking   14 minutes
This paper consists of **four parts**. The standard test format is two candidates and two examiners. One examiner takes part in the conversation while the other examiner listens. Both examiners give marks. Candidates will be given photographs and other visual and written material to look at and talk about. Sometimes candidates will talk with the other candidates, sometimes with the examiner and sometimes with both.

Grading

The overall FCE grade is based on the total score gained in all five papers. Each paper is weighted to 40 marks. Therefore, the five FCE papers total 200 marks, after weighting. It is not necessary to achieve a satisfactory level in all five papers in order to pass the examination. Certificates are given to candidates who pass the examination with grade A, B or C. A is the highest. D and E are failing grades. All candidates are sent a Statement of Results which includes a graphical profile of their performance in each paper and shows their relative performance in each one.

For further information on grading and results, go to the website (see page 5).

Test 1

PAPER 1   READING (1 hour)

Part 1

You are going to read an extract from a novel. For questions **1–8**, choose the answer (**A**, **B**, **C** or **D**) which you think fits best according to the text.

Mark your answers **on the separate answer sheet**.

Many trees in the Brackham area were brought down in the terrible storms that March. The town itself lost two great lime trees from the former market square. The disappearance of such prominent features had altered the appearance of the town centre entirely, to the annoyance of its more conservative inhabitants.

Among the annoyed, under more normal circumstances, would have been Chief Inspector Douglas Pelham, head of the local police force. But at the height of that week's storm, when the wind brought down even the mature walnut tree in his garden, Pelham had in fact been in no fit state to notice. A large and healthy man, he had for the first time in his life been seriously ill with an attack of bronchitis.

When he first complained of an aching head and tightness in his chest, his wife, Molly, had tried to persuade him to go to the doctor. Convinced that the police force could not do without him, he had, as usual, ignored her and attempted to carry on working. Predictably, though he wouldn't have listened to anyone who tried to tell him so, this had the effect of fogging his memory and shortening his temper.

line 16 It was only when his colleague, Sergeant Lloyd, took the initiative and drove him to the doctor's door that he finally gave in. By that time, he didn't have the strength left to argue with her. In no time at all, she was taking him along to the chemist's to get his prescribed antibiotics and then home to his unsurprised wife who sent him straight to bed.

When Molly told him, on the Thursday morning, that the walnut tree had been brought down during the night, Pelham hadn't been able to take it in. On Thursday evening, he had asked weakly about damage to the house, groaned thankfully when he heard there was none, and pulled the sheets over his head.

It wasn't until Saturday, when the antibiotics took effect, his temperature dropped and he got up, that he realised with a shock that the loss of the walnut tree had made a permanent difference to the appearance of the living-room. The Pelhams' large house stood in a sizeable garden. It had not come cheap, but even so Pelham had no regrets about buying it. The leafy garden had created an impression of privacy. Now, though, the storm had changed his outlook.

Previously, the view from the living-room had featured the handsome walnut tree. This had not darkened the room because there was also a window on the opposite wall, but it had provided interesting patterns of light and shade that disguised the true state of the worn furniture that the family had brought with them from their previous house.

line 33 With the tree gone, the room seemed cruelly bright, its worn furnishings exposed in all their shabbiness. And the view from the window didn't bear looking at. The tall house next door, previously hidden by the tree, was now there, dominating the outlook with its unattractive purple bricks and external pipes. It seemed to have a great many upstairs windows, all of them watching the Pelhams' every movement.

'Doesn't it look terrible?' Pelham croaked to his wife.

But Molly, standing in the doorway, sounded more pleased than dismayed. 'That's what I've been telling you ever since we came here. We have to buy a new sofa, whatever it costs.'

1 Why were some people in Brackham annoyed after the storm?

   A The town looked different.
   B The police had done little to help.
   C No market could be held.
   D Fallen trees had not been removed.

2 In the third paragraph, what do we learn about Chief Inspector Pelham's general attitude to his work?

   A He finds it extremely annoying.
   B He is sure that he fulfils a vital role.
   C He considers the systems are not clear enough.
   D He does not trust the decisions made by his superiors.

3 Who does 'her' in line 16 refer to?

   A Molly Pelham
   B the doctor
   C the chemist
   D Sergeant Lloyd

4 When Inspector Pelham's wife first told him about the walnut tree, he appeared to be

   A worried.
   B shocked.
   C saddened.
   D uninterested.

5 What aspect of the Pelhams' furniture does 'shabbiness' in line 33 describe?

   A its colour
   B its condition
   C its position
   D its design

6 As a result of the storm, the Pelhams' living-room

   A was pleasantly lighter.
   B felt less private.
   C had a better view.
   D was in need of repair.

7 Why did Molly sound pleased by her husband's comment?

   A It proved that he was well again.
   B She agreed about the tree.
   C She thought he meant the sofa.
   D It was what she expected him to say.

8 From what we learn of Inspector Pelham, he could best be described as

   A open-minded.
   B well-liked.
   C warm-hearted.
   D strong-willed.

Part 2

You are going to read a magazine interview with a sportswoman. Seven sentences have been removed from the article. Choose from the sentences **A–H** the one which fits each gap (**9–15**). There is one extra sentence which you do not need to use.

Mark your answers **on the separate answer sheet**.

The Netball Captain

In our series on women in sport, Suzie Ellis went to meet England's netball captain.

Kendra Slawinski is captain of England's netball team. When I met her, she'd had a typical day for the weeks leading up to next month's World Championships: a day's teaching at a local school followed by a training session in the local supermarket car park.

I was surprised to hear about her training venue.

'Don't you get strange looks?' I asked her. 'I'm too involved in what I'm doing – concentrating on my movements and my feet – to see anything else,' she said. 'I might notice cars slow down out of the corner of my eye, but that's all.'

'My whole life now is all about making sure I'm at my absolute best for the Championships,' says Kendra. '[9] B'. These are her fourth World Championships and they are guaranteed to be the biggest ever, with 27 nations taking part.

'We'll have home support behind us, which is so special,' she says. 'And it's important that the reputation of netball in this country should be improved. [10] H A home crowd will have expectations and give more support. People will expect us to start the tournament with a good game.'

Their first game is against Barbados and it comes immediately after the opening ceremony. '[11] F They have lots of ability.'

The England team are currently ranked fourth in the world. But, as Kendra points out, the World Championships will be tough. 'You have to push yourself to play each day, there's no rest between games as in a series. And you can still win an international series if you lose the first game. [12] A',

In the fifteen years since she has been playing at top level, the sport has become harder, faster. On court, players are more aggressive. 'You don't do all that training not to come out a winner,' says Kendra.

'[13] C We're all friendlier after the game.'

Netball is also taking a far more scientific approach to fitness testing.

'It is essential that we all think and train like world-class players,' says Kendra.

'[14] G I see my role as supporting and encouraging the rest of the team.'

'From the very beginning, my netball career has always been carefully planned,' she says. '[15] D'

Doubtless she will coach young players in the future, but at the moment her eyes are firmly set on her last big event. As she leads out her team in the opening candlelight ceremony, she is more than likely to have a tear in her eye. Her loyal supporters will be behind her every step of the way.

A But the Championships are different because there's only one chance and you have to be ready to make the most of it.

B In fact, some of them help me with my speed and ball-skills training.

C But once the final whistle blows, you become a different person.

D So I took the decision some time ago that this competition would be the end of it as far as playing is concerned.

E I'm on a strict timetable to gain maximum fitness for them.

F As far as I'm aware, we have always beaten them, but they'll be exciting to play.

G As captain, I think it's important that I have a strong mental attitude and lead by example.

H As a result of playing here, there will be more pressure than we're used to.

Part 3

You are going to read a magazine article about five young designers. For questions **16–30**, choose from the designers (**A–E**). The designers may be chosen more than once. When more than one answer is required, these may be given in any order.

Mark your answers **on the separate answer sheet**.

___

Which designer(s)

advises against certain styles?	**16** E	
took a business decision based on their own personal taste?	**17** B	
had begun designing before being trained?	**18** A	
have adapted a traditional style?	**19** A	**20** B
works in a variety of environments?	**21** E	
is working with a material which is new to them?	**22** C	
have used their reputation to develop a new area of business?	**23** D	**24** A
are completely self-taught?	**25** C	**26** E
mention how tastes have changed recently?	**27** D	**28** C
have received professional recognition?	**29** D	**30** B

Style Merchants

Style informs every part of our lives today from clothes to interior decoration and accessories. Jo Foley provides a taste of the trends for this year's followers of fashion.

A Ned Ingham: Dress Designer

Ned Ingham makes dreamy, romantic wedding dresses. 'People would do well to avoid the traditional, rather stiff dresses and the 'frilly' look in favour of much simpler styles,' he explains. Ingham has been drawing and designing wedding dresses since he was a schoolboy. Then, at the age of 16, he enrolled at fashion school, where he gained the technical skills to cut and construct clothes. But you do not have to be a bride to own an Ingham dress: he also designs long, classic evening dresses, given a fresh touch by up-to-the-minute colours and fabrics. For the less adventurous, Ingham's designs include a classic summer navy-blue suit, the centrepiece of the Englishwoman's wardrobe for most of the 20th century. But in his hands, it looks as new as tomorrow.

B Sally Quail: Jeweller

Although she once worked for an art dealer, Sally Quail has had no formal training in jewellery. It was only when she could not find an engagement ring she liked that she decided to design her own. The resulting enquiries encouraged her to set up as a designer in 1990. Now her pieces are sought out by many stars of stage and screen. Her signature style is large semi-precious stones set in gold to make magnificent necklaces, bracelets and rings fashioned after those worn in the 18th century. However, she has recently begun to use the most precious stone of all – diamonds. 'It must reflect my age,' says 36-year-old Quail. 'I reached that moment in every woman's life when she wants a diamond and that is when I began working with them.'

C Lily Grimson: Handbag Designer

Just four years after setting up in the fiercely competitive fashion business, Lily Grimson, with only an introductory course in art and design behind her, has had two of her creations selected for a major design exhibition. Whatever the shape and form of her designs, they are never ignored. All of Grimson's fashion bags are handmade in the UK. The Grimson handbag is not simply a container – the bags are full of glamour, whether fashioned from the finest calfskin or the heaviest silk. A combination of chic and care makes a Grimson bag something special.

D Peter Little: Hairdresser

For over 20 years, Peter Little has taken his scissors to some of the world's top heads. Everyone who is anyone has had their hair styled by this man. 'Most women want real-looking hair and a style they can manage at home,' he says. So his approach is a novel one – to ensure that his clients never appear as if they have just walked out of a salon. But this carefree attitude and casual look does not come cheap – £250 for the first appointment, and there's a three-month waiting list. Trading on his celebrity, Peter has produced his own range of hairdryers and other styling equipment. Now, those who can't make it to his salon can create their own styles back at home.

E Penny Pratt: Florist

In addition to running her tiny shop, Penny Pratt is a flower consultant for a large chain of supermarkets and provides floral ideas to a number of top restaurants. All of this is good going for someone who has no floristry qualifications and gave up her job as a teacher 10 years ago in order to do 'something different'. And her simple, yet incredibly modern, creations have begun to capture every design prize in the flower business, which has helped her in setting up her own London Flower School. She has recently combined her skills on extremely successful lecture trips to Japan and the USA. She says, 'Flower arrangements are much simpler these days. Keep them simple but strong and don't have too many leaves – they are too large and architectural. For wedding bouquets, whatever your arrangement, the golden rule remains: the flowers must be of the same species.'

PAPER 2   WRITING (1 hour 20 minutes)

Part 1

You **must** answer this question. Write your answer in **120–150** words in an appropriate style.

---

1   You are helping to organise a visit to a college in an English-speaking country for a group of students. You have received a letter from Michael Slater, the College Director. Read the letter and the notes you have made. Then write a letter to Mr Slater using **all** your notes.

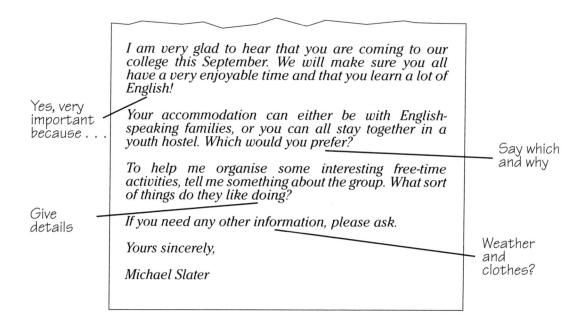

I am very glad to hear that you are coming to our college this September. We will make sure you all have a very enjoyable time and that you learn a lot of English!

Your accommodation can either be with English-speaking families, or you can all stay together in a youth hostel. Which would you prefer?

To help me organise some interesting free-time activities, tell me something about the group. What sort of things do they like doing?

If you need any other information, please ask.

Yours sincerely,

Michael Slater

Yes, very important because . . .

Say which and why

Give details

Weather and clothes?

Write your **letter**. You must use grammatically correct sentences with accurate spelling and punctuation in a style appropriate for the situation.

Do not write any postal addresses.

Part 2

Write an answer to **one** of the questions **2–5** in this part. Write your answer in **120–180** words in an appropriate style.

---

2 Your English class has done a project on transport. Your teacher has now asked you to write an essay giving your opinions on the following statement.

There is no future for public transport because travelling by car is so much more convenient.

Write your **essay**.

3 You see this announcement in your school English-language magazine.

> ### New Clubs after School
>
> Your school wants to start some new after-school clubs. Chess, table tennis, guitar playing and cookery have been suggested as possible ideas for clubs. What do you think? Write us an article for the school magazine.
> - Tell us which one of these four ideas you like best **and** why.
> - Make one other suggestion for a new club **and** explain why it would be a good idea.

Write your **article**.

4 You recently saw this notice in an international travel magazine.

> ### Reviews needed
>
> We would like our readers to send us reviews of good or bad hotels. Write about a hotel anywhere in the world. In your review, describe the hotel and say why you did or did not enjoy staying there.
>
> We will publish the most interesting reviews.

Write your **review**.

5 Answer **one** of the following two questions based on **one** of the titles below.

(a) *Officially Dead* – Richard Prescott

You have had a class discussion on the robbery in *Officially Dead*. Now your teacher has asked you to write an essay answering this question:

*'Why did the police suspect John and Linda Bentley **and** how were they eventually caught?'*

Write your **essay**.

(b) *Pride and Prejudice* – Jane Austen

You have received this letter from your English penfriend, Greg.

> *Pride and Prejudice* has so many different characters! Which person do you feel the most sympathy for and why? Write and tell me.
> Greg

Write your **letter** to Greg.

PAPER 3 USE OF ENGLISH (45 minutes)

Part 1

For questions **1–12**, read the text below and decide which answer (**A**, **B**, **C** or **D**) best fits each gap. There is an example at the beginning (**0**).

Mark your answers **on the separate answer sheet**.

Example:

0 A learn   **B** capture   **C** discover   **D** get

0	A	B	C	D
	—	–	–	–

Learning to make a perfect pizza

According to the European Pizza-Makers' Association, making a good pizza is not a straightforward skill to **(0)** ..... . The ingredients seem very simple: flour, yeast, water and a bit of salt. **(1)** ..... , water and flour can easily **(2)** ..... a rather unappetizing gluey mix, and anyone who has eaten a **(3)** ..... quality pizza will know how bad it can make your stomach **(4)** ..... .

'In Italy, 70 per cent of pizza makers could improve on their product, not to **(5)** ..... all the pizza makers around the world who **(6)** ..... uneatable meals,' says Antonio Primiceri, the Association's founder. He has now started a pizza school in an attempt to **(7)** ..... the reputation of this traditional dish. As part of an **(8)** ..... course, the students at Mr Primiceri's school are taught to **(9)** ..... common mistakes, produce a good basic mixture, add a tasty topping and cook the pizza properly. 'Test the finished pizza by breaking the crust,' advises Mr Primiceri. 'If the soft **(10)** ..... inside the pizza is white, clean and dry, it's a good pizza. If it is not like this, the pizza will **(11)** ..... your stomach. You will feel **(12)** ..... full and also thirsty.'

1 **A** However   **B** Despite   **C** Although   **D** Conversely

2 **A** make out   **B** take up   **C** put out   **D** turn into

3 **A** sad   **B** poor   **C** short   **D** weak

4 **A** sense   **B** do   **C** feel   **D** be

5 **A** state   **B** mention   **C** remark   **D** tell

6 **A** submit   **B** give   **C** provide   **D** deal

7 **A** save   **B** hold   **C** deliver   **D** return

8 **A** extensive   **B** extreme   **C** intensive   **D** intentional

9 **A** pass   **B** escape   **C** miss   **D** avoid

10 **A** spot   **B** part   **C** side   **D** slice

11 **A** worry   **B** upset   **C** ache   **D** depress

12 **A** discouragingly   **B** tightly   **C** uncomfortably   **D** heavily

Part 2

For questions **13–24**, read the text below and think of the word which best fits each gap. Use only **one** word in each gap. There is an example at the beginning (**0**).

Write your answers **IN CAPITAL LETTERS on the separate answer sheet**.

Example: | **0** | *I* | *T* | | | | | | | | | | | | | | | | |

Hollywood

How was (**0**) ....*it*......that Hollywood came to be the place everyone associates with the American film industry?

In 1887, Harvey Wilcox, a property developer, bought a house and all the surrounding land on a hillside in southern California. His wife overheard a woman talking on a train about her summer house, (**13**) *which* she called 'Hollywood'. Mrs Wilcox liked the name (**14**) *so* much that she decided to give her new home (**15**) *the* same name. Mr Wilcox then built other houses on his land and used the name for the whole community.

In normal circumstances most people (**16**) *would* never have heard of Hollywood. But between 1908 and 1913 (**17**) *something* else happened. Many small independent film companies began moving to southern California (**18**) *for* two main reasons. Firstly, they were having problems (**19**) *with* the larger, more powerful studios in New York. Secondly, they were attracted by the sunny climate, which let them film throughout the year (**20**) *without* the need for expensive lighting.

Only one studio actually set (**21**) *up* in Hollywood itself, because the local people took legal measures (**22**) *that to* prevent any more from arriving. The other studios that came to the area were all built outside Hollywood. Nevertheless, by 1915 'Hollywood' (**23**) *had* become familiar as a term for the movie business (**24**) *as* a whole.

$\frac{11}{12}$

Part 3

For questions **25–34**, read the text below. Use the word given in capitals at the end of some of the lines to form a word that fits in the gap **in the same line**. There is an example at the beginning (**0**).

Write your answers **IN CAPITAL LETTERS on the separate answer sheet**.

Example:

0	M	E	E	T	I	N	G								

A new supermarket for the town

At a public (**0**) ...~~meeting~~... held recently, residents of the town of Oxwell   **MEET**

met local politicians and shop owners to discuss plans to build a large

supermarket in the town. A wide (**25**) ...variety... of opinions was   **VARY**

expressed, some in favour and some against the project. A

(**26**) ...director... of the supermarket group, who was present at the meeting,   **DIRECT**

stated that the supermarket would benefit the (**27**) ...inhabitants... of   **INHABIT**

Oxwell as it would give people more (**28**) ...choices... when shopping. He   **CHOOSE**

also pointed out that it would lead to a (**29**) ...growth... in the number of   **GROW**

jobs available in the town, which has a high rate of (**30**) ...employees... ✗ ~~unemployment~~   **EMPLOY**

Although there was general (**31**) ...agreement... on the need for new jobs,   **AGREE**

some of those present claimed that the presence of the proposed new

supermarket would actually lead to the (**32**) ...loses... ✗ ~~loss~~ of jobs. They   **LOSE**

pointed out that small shops would be forced to close as they would

be (**33**) ...unable... to compete with supermarket prices. The final   **ABLE**

(**34**) ...decision... on whether or not to build the supermarket will be made   **DECIDE**

next month.

Part 4

For questions **35–42**, complete the second sentence so that it has a similar meaning to the first sentence, using the word given. **Do not change the word given.** You must use between **two** and **five** words, including the word given. Here is an example (**0**).

Example:

0   You must do exactly what the manager tells you.

CARRY

You must .... instructions exactly.

The gap can be filled by the words 'carry out the manager's', so you write:

Example:	0	*CARRY OUT THE MANAGER'S*

Write **only** the missing words **IN CAPITAL LETTERS on the separate answer sheet**.

---

35   We had to finish all the work before we could leave.

UNTIL

We had to stay ..until..we.~~are~~..finished.... all the work.
(had)

36   Tim had not expected the concert to be so good.

BETTER

The concert ..was.better.than.Tim'.. had expected.

37   If Cheryl doesn't train harder, she'll never get into the swimming team.

DOES

Cheryl will never get into the swimming team ..if only she does.. ✗ more training.
(unless she does)

38   'Do you realise what the time is, Steve?' asked Chris.

WHAT

Chris asked Steve ..what time.. it was.
(whether he realised)

39 The company decided to advertise the job in a national newspaper.

PUT

The company decided to .....put some advertisement....... the job in a national
newspaper.

[handwritten: an ... about]

40 At the end of his speech, the winner thanked his parents.

FINISHED

The winner .....had finished by thanking...... his parents.

[handwritten: x finished his speech before thanking.]

41 I applied for the job a month ago.

MONTH

It .....was a month since........... I applied for the job.

42 They received many letters of support after they had appeared on television.

FOLLOWING

They received many letters of support .....after the following appearance......
on television.

[handwritten: their]

PAPER 4   LISTENING (approximately 40 minutes)

Part 1

You will hear people talking in eight different situations. For questions **1–8**, choose the best answer (**A**, **B** or **C**).

---

1   You hear part of a radio play.
   Where is the scene taking place?

   A   in the street

   B   in a bank

   C   in a police station

2   You overhear the beginning of a lecture.
   What subject are the students taking?

   A   medicine

   B   sport

   C   music

3   You overhear a conversation in a college.
   Who is the young man?

   A   a new student

   B   a student in the middle of a course

   C   a former student

4   You hear a woman on the radio talking about a cookbook.
   What does she regret?

   A   not looking after it

   B   not having kept it

   C   not using it properly

5 You hear someone talking about the day he met someone famous.
How did he feel after meeting Chris Turner?

  A unimpressed with the footballer

  B angry with his friend

  C disappointed with himself

6 You hear a woman talking on the phone.
Why has she called?

  A to request a meeting

  B to offer assistance

  C to apologise for her absence

7 You overhear an extract from a radio play.
What is the young woman's relationship with the man?

  A She's a pupil of his.

  B She's a relative of his.

  C She's a patient of his.

8 You hear someone telling a story about a strange thing that happened in the mountains.
What point does the story prove?

  A how strange things can be explained simply

  B how easy it is to imagine things

  C how you can be tricked by the silence

Part 2

You will hear part of a talk about dolls. For questions **9–18**, complete the sentences.

Dolls

The first known dolls were found in [_____ **9**] in ancient Egypt.

The earliest dolls in the museum date from the [_____ **10**]

Early European dolls were dressed like [_____ **11**]

On the 17th-century dolls, you can see details like the [_____ **12**]

17th-century dolls may cost as much as [_____ **13**] each.

Collectors look for examples in perfect condition, with their

[_____ **14**]

19th-century dolls had [_____ **15**] and real hair.

If you can take off the doll's hair, you may see the

[_____ **16**] underneath.

Before the 20th century, all dolls were [_____ **17**], not babies.

From the 1930s, dolls were made of [_____ **18**]

Part 3

You will hear five different people talking about why they decided to become nurses. For questions **19–23**, choose which of the reasons (**A–F**) each speaker is giving. Use the letters only once. There is one extra letter which you do not need to use.

A   It was a childhood dream.

| | Speaker 1 | | 19 |

B   Teachers had recommended it.

| | Speaker 2 | | 20 |

C   A friend had decided to do it.

| | Speaker 3 | | 21 |

D   It offered a secure income.

| | Speaker 4 | | 22 |

E   It is a family tradition.

| | Speaker 5 | | 23 |

F   It is emotionally satisfying.

Part 4

You will hear an interview with someone who works in the film industry. For questions **24–30**, choose the best answer (**A**, **B** or **C**).

24 What does Alan say about his job title?

 A It confuses a lot of people.

 B It is just a name for the job.

 C It encourages him to work hard.

25 Alan considers his job to be

 A creative.

 B managerial.

 C administrative.

26 When he started in films, Alan

 A immediately learnt new skills.

 B did the same kind of work as before.

 C had to change his working methods.

27 When Alan was working on his latest film,

 A problems were caused by the weather.

 B there were difficulties moving the equipment.

 C he wished he was in the studio.

28 For Alan, the disadvantage of the job is

 A the amount of responsibility.

 B the criticism he receives.

 C the effect on family life.

29 For a job like this, Alan recommends

    A   studying to be an electrician.

    B   getting a qualification in maths.

    C   doing a course in film production.

30 In thinking about the future, Alan wants to

    A   face different problems.

    B   work in other areas of production.

    C   continue doing the same job.

PAPER 5   SPEAKING (14 minutes)

You take the Speaking test with another candidate, referred to here as your partner. There are two examiners. One will speak to you and your partner and the other will be listening. Both examiners will award marks.

Part 1 (3 minutes)

The examiner asks you and your partner questions about yourselves. You may be asked about things like 'your home town', 'your interests', 'your career plans', etc.

Part 2 (a one-minute 'long turn' for each candidate, plus 20-second response from the second candidate)

The examiner gives you two photographs and asks you to talk about them for one minute. The examiner then asks your partner a question about your photographs and your partner responds briefly.

Then the examiner gives your partner two different photographs. Your partner talks about these photographs for one minute. This time the examiner asks you a question about your partner's photographs and you respond briefly.

Part 3 (approximately 3 minutes)

The examiner asks you and your partner to talk together. You may be asked to solve a problem or try to come to a decision about something. For example, you might be asked to decide the best way to use some rooms in a language school. The examiner gives you a picture to help you but does not join in the conversation.

Part 4 (approximately 4 minutes)

The interlocutor asks some further questions, which leads to a more general discussion of what you have talked about in Part 3. You may comment on your partner's answers if you wish.

Test 2

PAPER 1   READING (1 hour)

Part 1

You are going to read an extract from a novel. For questions **1–8**, choose the answer (**A**, **B**, **C** or **D**) which you think fits best according to the text.

Mark your answers **on the separate answer sheet**.

On Saturday mornings I worked in the family shop. I started cycling down to the shop with Dad on Saturdays as soon as I was big enough. I thought of it as giving him a hand and so I didn't mind what I did, although it was mostly just fetching and carrying at a run all morning. I managed not to think of it as work and I looked forward to the bar of chocolate my grandmother passed me unsmilingly as I left. I tried not to look at her; I had reason to feel guilty because I'd generally already eaten some dried fruits or a sliver of cheese when no one was looking. As soon as I was fifteen, though, Dad said, 'That's it, our Janet. You're of working age now and you're not coming to work unless your grandmother pays you properly.' He did his best to make his chin look determined. 'I shall speak to her.'

The next Saturday, Gran called me into her little office behind the shop. I always hated going in there. She had an electric heater on full blast, and the windows were always kept tightly closed whatever the weather. There were piles of dusty catalogues and brochures on the floor. 'You're wanting to get paid, I hear,' Gran said. 'Yes, please,' I replied. It was rather like visiting the headmistress at school, so I was very quiet and respectful. Gran searched through the mess of papers on her crowded desk, sighing and clicking her tongue. Eventually she produced an official-looking leaflet and ran her fingers along the columns of figures. 'How old are you?' 'Fifteen … Gran,' I added for extra politeness, but she looked at me as if I had been cheeky. 'Full-timers at your age get forty pounds for a thirty-five-hour week,' she announced in such a way as to leave no doubt that she wasn't in favour of this. 'No wonder there's no profit in shopkeeping! So, Janet, what's that per hour?' Questions like that always flustered me. Instead of trying to work them out in my head, I would just stand there, unable to think straight. 'I'll get a pencil and paper,' I offered. 'Don't bother,' snapped Gran angrily, 'I'll do it myself. I'll give you a pound an hour; take it or leave it.' 'I'll take it, please.' 'And I expect real work for it, mind. No standing about, and if I catch you eating any of the stock, there'll be trouble. That's theft, and it's a crime.'

From then on, my main job at the shop was filling the shelves. This was dull, but I hardly expected to be trusted with handling the money. Once or twice, however, when Dad was extra busy, I'd tried to help him by serving behind the counter. I hated it. It was very difficult to remember the prices of everything and I was particularly hopeless at using the till. Certain customers made unkind remarks about this, increasing my confusion and the chances of my making a fool of myself.

It was an old-established village shop, going back 150 years at least and it was really behind the times even then. Dad longed to be able to make the shop more attractive to customers, but Gran wouldn't hear of it. I overheard them once arguing about whether to buy a freezer cabinet. 'Our customers want frozen food,' Dad said. 'They see things advertised and if they can't get them from us, they'll go elsewhere.' 'Your father always sold fresh food,' Gran replied. 'People come here for quality, they don't want all that frozen stuff.'

Actually, she gave way in the end over the freezer. Mr Timson, her great rival, installed one in his shop at the other end of the village and customers started making loud comments about how handy it was, being able to get frozen food in the village, and how good Mr Timson's sausages were. That really upset her because she was proud of her sausages and she ungraciously gave Dad the money to buy the freezer. Within a couple of weeks, she was eating frozen food like the rest of us.

1   How did Janet feel when she first started her Saturday morning job?

   A   She enjoyed the work that she was given.
   B   She was pleased to be helping her father.
   C   She worried that she was not doing it well.
   D   She was only really interested in the reward.

2   What do we learn about her grandmother's office in the second paragraph?

   A   It needed decorating.
   B   It was untidy.
   C   It had too much furniture in it.
   D   It was dark.

3   'This' (line 19) refers to

   A   shopkeepers' profits.
   B   a thirty-five-hour week.
   C   Janet's request.
   D   the recommended wage.

4   'Flustered' (line 20) means

   A   bored.
   B   angered.
   C   confused.
   D   depressed.

5   Why did Janet's grandmother react angrily to her offer to fetch a pencil and paper?

   A   Janet was unable to answer her question.
   B   Janet had been unwilling to help her.
   C   Janet had made an unhelpful suggestion.
   D   Janet had answered her rudely.

6   What did Janet's father and grandmother disagree about?

   A   how to keep their customers loyal to the shop
   B   the type of advertising needed to attract customers
   C   the type of customers they needed to attract
   D   how to get new customers to come to the shop

7   What eventually persuaded Janet's grandmother to buy a freezer?

   A   She found that she liked frozen food after all.
   B   A new shop opening in the village had one.
   C   It was suggested that her products weren't fresh.
   D   She responded to pressure from her customers.

8   What impression do we get of Janet's feelings towards her grandmother?

   A   She respected her fairness.
   B   She doubted her judgement.
   C   She disliked her manner.
   D   She admired her determination.

Part 2

You are going to read an article written by someone who lives in a house in a valley. Seven sentences have been removed from the article. Choose from the sentences **A–H** the one which fits each gap (**9–15**). There is one extra sentence which you do not need to use.

Mark your answers **on the separate answer sheet**.

LIVING IN THE VALLEY

We had been living in our valley for sixteen months when we first realised the dangers that could exist in the surrounding hills and threaten our very survival.

9 **H** Until that time, we had felt safe and sheltered in our valley below the protecting hills.

Soon snow began to fall. Within a day it lay some 15 centimetres deep. **10** **F** But on the neighbouring heights the snow was much deeper and stayed for longer. Up there the wind blasted fiercely. Deep in our valley we felt only sudden gusts of wind; trees swayed but the branches held firm.

And yet we knew that there was reason for us to worry. The snow and wind were certainly inconvenient but they did not really trouble us greatly. **11** **A** It reminded us of what could have occurred if circumstances had been different, if the flow of water from the hills had not, many years before, been controlled, held back by a series of dams.

In a short time the snow started to melt. Day after day, we watched furious clouds pile up high over the hills to the west. Sinister grey clouds extended over the valleys. **12** **E** We had seen enough of the sky; now we began to watch the river, which every day was becoming fuller and wilder.

The snow was gradually washed away as more and more rain streamed from the clouds, but high up in the hills the reservoir was filling and was fast approaching danger level. And then it happened – for the first time in years the reservoir overflowed. **13** **D**

The river seemed maddened as the waters poured almost horizontally down to its lower stretches. Just a couple of metres from our cottage, the stream seemed wild beneath the bridge. **14** **C** For three days we prayed that it would stay below its wall. Fortunately, our prayers were answered as the dam held and the waters began to subside.

On many occasions through the centuries before the dam was built, the river had flooded the nearby villages in just such a rage. Now, though, the dam restricts the flow of the river and usually all is well; the great mass of water from the hills, the product of snow and torrential rain, remains behind its barrier with just the occasional overflow. **15** **G** Thanks to this protection we can feel our home in the valley is still secure and safe.

A It was the river, the Ryburn, which normally flowed so gently, that threatened us most.

B And yet the immense power of all this water above us prevents us from ever believing ourselves to be completely safe in our home.

C They twisted and turned, rising eastwards and upwards, warning of what was to come.

D It was far deeper than we'd ever seen it so near our home, lunging furiously at its banks.

E We can thus enjoy, rather than fear, the huge clouds that hang over the valley, and can be thrilled by the tremendous power which we know the river possesses.

F It almost completely blocked our lane and made the streamside path slippery and dangerous.

G There in the heights it was like the Niagara Falls, as the water surged over the edge of the dam and poured into the stream below.

H It was the year when the storms came early, before the calendar even hinted at winter, even before November was out.

Part 3

You are going to read a magazine article in which five people talk about their characters. For questions **16–30**, choose from the people (**A–E**). The people may be chosen more than once. When more than one answer is required, these may be given in any order.

Mark your answers **on the separate answer sheet**.

Which person or people state(s) the following?

I used to avoid giving my opinions at work.	**16**	
Taking time off for your professional development can make you feel more self-assured.	**17**	
I never thought I'd be a confident person.	**18**	
I'm not influenced by people's opinions of me.	**19**	
Everyone gets nervous at times.	**20**	**21**
Initially, I misunderstood what confidence was.	**22**	
I find making notes very supportive in my work.	**23**	
A certain event changed the course of my life.	**24**	**25**
I've worked on having a confident appearance.	**26**	
I am realistic about my abilities.	**27**	**28**
My behaviour helps others relax too.	**29**	
Getting things wrong can have a positive result.	**30**	

Confident people
What's their secret?

Confident people may look as though they were born that way, but most will tell you that it's a s[...]
learned because they had to. Nina Hathway asks five people how they did it.

A Jenny

When I left school I was very shy and I always thought I'd stay that way. I was about twenty-five when I was asked to help out at my daughter's school. I was sure I wouldn't cope, but I surprised myself by doing well and someone there suggested that I should do a university course.

There was a huge knot in my stomach the day I turned up for my first lecture. But my confidence gradually grew – I became more outgoing. Looking back, working at the school was the turning point in my life that has helped everything else fall into place.

B Michaela

It all started four years ago when my father became ill and I had to take over the family business. I was so scared, I went over the top and became a bit too aggressive and impatient. I thought that was what confident people were like, but gradually I learned otherwise. To be confident you've got to believe in yourself.

If things get too demanding for me at work, I don't let myself feel guilty if I save a number of tasks until the next day. When I'm confronted with something difficult, I tell myself that I've got nothing to lose. It's fear that makes you lack confidence, so I'm always having quiet chats with myself to put aside those fears!

C Lisa

People think I'm very confident but, in fact, the calmer I look, the more terrified I really am. I've had to develop the ability to look confident because it's the most vital thing in TV. Interviewing people has helped me realise that most – if not all – of us get tense in important situations, and we feel calmer when we speak to someone who's genuinely friendly. The best ever piece of advice came from my mother when I was agonising as a teenager about wearing the right clothes. She simply cried, 'Who's looking at you? Everybody's too busy worrying about how they look.' I've found that's well worth remembering.

I also think you gain confidence by tackling things that scare you. When I took my driving test I was so nervous, but I passed. After that I felt sure that I'd never feel so frightened again, and I never have.

D Barbara

My confidence comes naturally from really enjoying the work I do, but it's something that I've built up over the years. If you just get on with it and learn from any mistakes you make, you're more confident the next time round. I work hard and I'm popular in the restaurant, but it's probable that one out of ten people doesn't like me. I don't let that affect me. You've got to like yourself for what you are, not try to be what others expect.

My company runs a lot of training courses, and going on those has built up my self-esteem. The company also encourages employees to set manageable targets. It helps no end if you can see you're achieving something tangible, rather than reaching for the stars all at once, and ending up with nothing but air!

E Kim

After I left college I worked for years as a secretary and would sit in meetings, not always agreeing with what was being said, but too scared to speak up. Eventually, I summoned up the confidence to start making my point. Even so, when I first worked in politics, I'd never spoken in public before and always used to shake like a leaf. I would say to myself, 'Don't be so silly. People do this every day of their lives, so there's no reason why you can't.' I also found it helpful to jot a few things down to refer to – rather like having a comfort blanket!

I don't think there is anyone who isn't a little shaky when it comes to talking publicly. The real secret of confidence lies in telling yourself over and over again, 'Nothing is impossible.'

Part 1

You **must** answer this question. Write your answer in **120–150** words in an appropriate style.

1   Your English friend, Peter, has sent you an email asking you to help him organise a special
surprise birthday party for his sister, Anna. Read Peter's email and the notes you have made.
Then write an email to Peter using **all** your notes.

---

email

From:	Peter
Sent:	15th March
Subject:	Birthday party

---

*Sounds
good but
expensive*

We must make sure that Anna has no idea we're
planning such a great surprise! I'm not sure how many
people to invite but our house is certainly too small. Do
you think we should book the Majestic Hotel for the
evening and have the party there? Anna loves music so
we could have a live band.

I've also spent ages thinking about what we could all   *Anna enjoys*
buy her as a present. Do you have any ideas? —————— *travelling
so ....*

Could you come the day before the party to help with
the preparations? There's a lot to think about so I'd — *Sorry – busy
that day*
really like your help! And can you suggest something
else that will make this party really special?

*Yes, how
about ....*

Best wishes

Peter

Write your **email**. You must use grammatically correct sentences with accurate spelling and
punctuation in a style appropriate for the situation.

Part 2

Write an answer to **one** of the questions **2–5** in this part. Write your answer in **120–180** words in an appropriate style.

---

2   You have had a discussion on fashion in your English class. Your teacher has now asked you to write an essay, giving your opinions on the following statement:

Young people always want to dress differently from their parents.

Write your **essay**.

3   You have seen this advertisement for a job in the USA in an international magazine.

> **USA SUMMER CAMPS**
>
> If you can speak English and you are cheerful, energetic and hardworking, you are the right person for us. Food and accommodation are provided. You just pay the air fare.
>
> You will   – look after children aged 8 –12
>   – help organise sports and evening activities
>   – work in the kitchens
>
> Write to the director, Mrs Connor, and explain why you would be a suitable person for the job.

Write your **application**.

4   Your teacher has asked you to write a story for an international student magazine. The story must **begin** with the following words:

Michael closed the door and knew at that moment he had made a mistake.

Write your **story**.

5   Answer **one** of the following two questions based on **one** of the titles below.

(a) *Officially Dead* – Richard Prescott

You have seen this announcement in an English magazine.

> **TRUTH and LIES**
>
> We are looking for articles about books where telling the truth or lies is important to the story. The best articles will be published next month.

Write an **article** about the importance of truth and lies in *Officially Dead*.

(b) *Pride and Prejudice* – Jane Austen

Your English class has discussed the characters of Lizzy and Mr Darcy in *Pride and Prejudice*. Your teacher has now given you this essay for homework:

Explain how and why Lizzy's feelings for Mr Darcy change.

Write your **essay**.

PAPER 3   USE OF ENGLISH (45 minutes)

Part 1

For questions **1–12**, read the text below and decide which answer (**A, B, C** or **D**) best fits each gap. There is an example at the beginning (**0**).

Mark your answers **on the separate answer sheet**.

Example:

0 A celebrates   **B** shows   **C** honours   **D** demonstrates

---

Everyone's an artist

Every year, the village of Pettineo **(0)** ..... its unique arts festival. For a few days each summer, artists from all over Europe **(1)** ..... at this village near the north coast of Sicily to **(2)** ..... the creative atmosphere. During their stay, the artists get together with the local people to paint a one-kilometre long picture that runs the **(3)** ..... of the high street. **(4)** ..... the painting is done, each visiting artist joins a local family for a big lunch and, **(5)** ..... the meal, the family receives the **(6)** ..... of the painting that the artist has painted. As a result, **(7)** ..... few villagers are rich, almost every home has at least one painting by a well-known European artist. Visitors to the village are eagerly **(8)** ..... into homes to see these paintings.

The festival was the idea of Antonio Presti, a local businessman who **(9)** ..... it up several years ago. Since then, Pettineo has **(10)** ..... a sort of domestic art museum in **(11)** ..... any visitor can ring a doorbell, go into a house and **(12)** ..... a painting. In addition to this exhibition of paintings in people's homes, for those who have time to spare, there is an opportunity to wander through the display of huge sculptures in the village square.

1 **A** group **B** crowd **C** gather **D** combine

2 **A** amuse **B** enjoy **C** entertain **D** delight

3 **A** size **B** measure **C** length **D** area

4 **A** Just **B** Once **C** Soon **D** Only

5 **A** in addition to **B** in place of **C** in common with **D** in exchange for

6 **A** partition **B** section **C** division **D** region

7 **A** though **B** despite **C** since **D** even

8 **A** persuaded **B** invited **C** requested **D** attracted

9 **A** set **B** put **C** got **D** had

10 **A** become **B** advanced **C** grown **D** increased

11 **A** what **B** where **C** whom **D** which

12 **A** wonder **B** stare **C** admire **D** respect

Part 2

For questions **13–24**, read the text below and think of the word which best fits each gap. Use only **one** word in each gap. There is an example at the beginning **(0)**.

Write your answers **IN CAPITAL LETTERS on the separate answer sheet**.

Example: | 0 | W | I | T | H | | | | | | | | | | | | | | | |

Problems for actors

Many actors do not like working **(0)** ...with... children or animals. This is probably **(13)** why they are afraid that the audience may become **(14)** .less. interested in the children and animals than in them.

Actors can have problems **(15)** of.a different kind when they are required to eat or drink on stage. If they have **(16)** too... much food in their mouths, the words they say may not **(17)** ...be... clear, and they may even end up coughing or choking.

Other problems can occur with food **(18)** when. films are being made. In a recent film, during **(19)** which a family was waiting to have a meal, one of the actors entered with a large roast chicken on a tray and started cutting some meat from it while he was speaking. Having cut off a whole chicken leg he completely forgot **(20)** what. his next words were. The scene had to be filmed **(21)** again. This would not really have mattered **(22)** when there had been another roast chicken in the studio, but there was not. At **(23)** least, nobody knew what to do, but eventually the problem was solved **(24)** .by... putting a nail in the leg and attaching it back onto the chicken.

Part 3

For questions **25–34**, read the text below. Use the word given in capitals at the end of some of the lines to form a word that fits in the gap **in the same line**. There is an example at the beginning (**0**).

Write your answers **IN CAPITAL LETTERS on the separate answer sheet.**

Example:

0	G	R	O	W	T	H										

Airports

Because of the recent **(0)** ...growth... in air travel, airports have become more **GROW**

than ever before symbols of international importance. They therefore have

to look good and are **(25)** frequently .... designed by well-known architects. In **FREQUENT**

addition to this, competition and customer demand mean that airports

generally have to have **(26)** impressive .... facilities nowadays. For instance, **IMPRESS**

there are **(27)** comfortable .... departure lounges, where passengers can wait **COMFORT**

before their **(28)** fright .... takes off, luxurious restaurants, shopping areas **FLY**

and banks. Good road and rail **(29)** connection .... with nearby towns and cities **CONNECT**

are also essential, with large numbers of people needing to get to and from

the airport quickly and efficiently.

However, it is becoming **(30)** increasingly .... difficult to find land on which to **INCREASE**

build airports. One reason for this is that aircraft, despite **(31)** improvement **IMPROVE**

in engine design, are still very **(32)** noisy .... , and need a considerable **NOISE**

amount of space in which to land and take off. This of course means

that **(33)** crowded .... residential areas need to be avoided, so, **CROWD**

(34) unfortunately .... , travellers often find that the airport they need to use might **FORTUNATE**

be situated at an inconvenient distance from the city.

Part 4

For questions **35–42**, complete the second sentence so that it has a similar meaning to the first sentence, using the word given. **Do not change the word given**. You must use between **two** and **five** words, including the word given. Here is an example (**0**).

Example:

0   You must do exactly what the manager tells you.

CARRY

You must .... instructions exactly.

The gap can be filled by the words 'carry out the manager's', so you write:

Example:	0	*CARRY OUT THE MANAGER'S*

Write **only** the missing words **IN CAPITAL LETTERS on the separate answer sheet**.

---

35   John is interested in knowing more about astronomy.

LIKE

John ...~~would like to know~~..... more about astronomy.

36   Because of the parade, we weren't allowed to park in the High Street.

LET

Because of the parade, the police wouldn't ...~~let us park~~........................ in the High Street.

37   'Did you see that film on television on Saturday?' Susan asked me.

SEEN

Susan wanted to know ...~~if I had seen~~............... that film on television on Saturday.

38   'I'm afraid these jeans have a hole in them,' Tania told the shop assistant.

THERE

'I'm afraid that ...~~there is a hole in~~... these jeans,' Tania told the shop assistant.

39 Dan never takes any notice of my advice.

ATTENTION

Dan never ...*pay any attention to*... my advice.

40 'Can I borrow your bicycle, Sarah?' asked Frank.

LEND

Frank asked Sarah ...*if she could lend him*... her bicycle.

41 Maybe Peter forgot that we changed the time of the meeting.

MIGHT

Peter ...*might had forgot*... that we changed the time of the meeting.

42 All the children enjoy themselves at this summer camp.

FUN

Every ...*one had fun*... at this summer camp.

PAPER 4   LISTENING (approximately 40 minutes)

Part 1

You will hear people talking in eight different situations. For questions **1–8**, choose the best answer (**A**, **B** or **C**).

1   You overhear two people talking in a restaurant.
    Where has the woman just come from?

   A   a supermarket

   B   a hospital

   C   a football match

2   You hear a man talking about a mobile phone he has bought.
    What most attracted him to this phone?

   A   its size

   B   its reliability

   C   its price

3   You hear a man talking on the phone about buying a house.
    What is the purpose of his call?

   A   to apologise

   B   to complain

   C   to obtain information

4   You hear a teenage girl talking about her hobby.
    What is she talking about?

   A   a computer game

   B   a musical instrument

   C   a piece of sports equipment

5 On the news, you hear a story about a cat.
Where was the cat found?

A in a train carriage

B on the railway lines

C on a station platform

6 You hear a woman talking about how she gets ideas for her work.
Who is the woman?

A a novelist

B an artist

C a film-maker

7 You hear two people talking.
How does the woman feel?

A surprised

B satisfied

C relieved

8 You turn on the radio and hear a man speaking.
What are you listening to?

A a history programme

B a science-fiction story

C an advertisement

Part 2

You will hear part of a radio programme about bags for walkers. For questions **9–18**, complete the sentences.

Bags for walkers

Rod's shop sells bags and other [**9**] equipment.

A backpack could spoil your holiday if it doesn't [**10**]

A 35-litre bag is good for [**11**]

An upright bag is recommended for people who are going to [**12**]

To protect breakable items choose a bag with a [**13**]

A bag with [**14**] inside will allow you to separate your belongings.

External pockets can be used to carry tools that are [**15**] or dirty.

It is important that shoulder straps are [**16**]

A horizontal bar will prevent shoulder straps from [**17**]

Padded parts of the bag should have plenty of [**18**] so that sweat can escape.

Part 3

You will hear five different students who are studying away from home. They are talking about their accommodation. For questions **19–23**, choose from the list (**A–F**) what each speaker says about their accommodation. Use the letters only once. There is one extra letter which you do not need to use.

A I made a mistake there at first.

Speaker 1 | 19 |

B I was able to settle into a new area.

Speaker 2 | 20 |

C I had no choice in the matter.

Speaker 3 | 21 |

D I have recommended it to others.

Speaker 4 | 22 |

E There are more benefits than disadvantages.

Speaker 5 | 23 |

F I would prefer to have more freedom.

Part 4

You will hear part of a radio interview in which Tina White, a magazine editor, talks about her life and work. For questions **24–30**, choose the best answer (**A**, **B** or **C**).

24 In her first column, Tina chose to write about people who

    A   were very well known.

    B   had interesting ideas.

    C   lived in luxury.

25 She took up journalism because of

    A   her family connections.

    B   her father's support.

    C   her love for books.

26 Under her management, the magazine *Female Focus*

    A   reduced its losses.

    B   changed its image.

    C   made a profit.

27 She believes people are more likely to read an article if

    A   it has a good beginning.

    B   its content is challenging.

    C   it is mentioned on the cover.

28 When she started her present job five years ago, she

    A   organised her ideal team.

    B   had more time to read everything.

    C   lacked confidence in her staff.

29 Tina says that she would be worried if she

    A   was criticised by the public.

    B   lost the respect of colleagues.

    C   lost her job.

30 In the future, she would like to

    A   be a book editor.

    B   produce a film.

    C   write fiction.

PAPER 5   SPEAKING (14 minutes)

You take the Speaking test with another candidate, referred to here as your partner. There are two examiners. One will speak to you and your partner and the other will be listening. Both examiners will award marks.

Part 1 (3 minutes)

The examiner asks you and your partner questions about yourselves. You may be asked about things like 'your home town', 'your interests', 'your career plans', etc.

Part 2 (a one-minute 'long turn' for each candidate, plus 20-second response from the second candidate)

The examiner gives you two photographs and asks you to talk about them for one minute. The examiner then asks your partner a question about your photographs and your partner responds briefly.

Then the examiner gives your partner two different photographs. Your partner talks about these photographs for one minute. This time the examiner asks you a question about your partner's photographs and you respond briefly.

Part 3 (approximately 3 minutes)

The examiner asks you and your partner to talk together. You may be asked to solve a problem or try to come to a decision about something. For example, you might be asked to decide the best way to use some rooms in a language school. The examiner gives you a picture to help you but does not join in the conversation.

Part 4 (approximately 4 minutes)

The interlocutor asks some further questions, which leads to a more general discussion of what you have talked about in Part 3. You may comment on your partner's answers if you wish.

Test 3

PAPER 1   READING (1 hour)

Part 1

You are going to read an article about a man who makes works of art out of seashells. For questions **1–8**, choose the answer (**A**, **B**, **C** or **D**) which you think fits best according to the text.

Mark your answers **on the separate answer sheet**.

THE SHELL ARTIST

At the age of 83 Peter Cooke has become a master of his art.

There are still many things that Peter Cooke would like to try his hand at – paper-making and feather-work are on his list. For the moment though, he will stick to the skill that he has been delighted to perfect over the past ten years: making delicate and unusual objects out of shells.

'Tell me if I am boring you,' he says, as he leads me round his apartment showing me his work. There is a fine line between being a bore and being an enthusiast, but Cooke need not worry: he fits into the latter category, helped both by his charm and by the beauty of the things he makes.

He points to a pair of shell-covered ornaments above a fireplace. 'I shan't be at all bothered if people don't buy them because I have got so used to them, and to me they're adorable. I never meant to sell my work commercially. Some friends came to see me about five years ago and said, "You must have an exhibition – people ought to see these. We'll talk to a man who owns an art gallery".' The result was an exhibition in London, at which 70 per cent of the objects were sold. His second exhibition opened at the gallery yesterday. Considering the enormous prices the pieces command – around £2,000 for the ornaments – an empty space above the fireplace would seem a small sacrifice for Cooke to make.

line 25

There are 86 pieces in the exhibition, with prices starting at £225 for a shell-flower in a crystal vase. Cooke insists that he has nothing to do with the prices and is cheerily open about their level: he claims there is nobody else in the world who produces work like his, and, as the gallery-owner told him, 'Well, you're going to stop one day and everybody will want your pieces because there won't be any more.'

'I do wish, though,' says Cooke, 'that I'd taken this up a lot earlier, because then I would have been able to produce really wonderful things – at least the potential would have been there. Although the ideas are still there and I'm doing the best I can now, I'm more limited physically than I was when I started.' Still, the work that he has managed to produce is a long way from the common shell constructions that can be found in seaside shops. 'I have a miniature mind,' he says, and this has resulted in boxes covered in thousands of tiny shells, little shaded pictures made from shells and baskets of astonishingly realistic flowers.

Cooke has created his own method and uses materials as and when he finds them. He uses the cardboard sent back with laundered shirts for his flower bases, a nameless glue bought in bulk from a sail-maker ('If it runs out, I don't know what I will do!') and washing-up liquid to wash the shells. 'I have an idea of what I want to do, and it just does itself,' he says of his working method, yet the attention to detail, colour gradations and symmetry he achieves look far from accidental.

Cooke's quest for beautiful, and especially tiny, shells has taken him further than his Norfolk shore: to France, Thailand, Mexico, South Africa and the Philippines, to name but a few of the beaches where he has lain on his stomach and looked for beauties to bring home. He is insistent that he only collects dead shells and defends himself against people who write him letters accusing him of stripping the world's beaches. 'When I am collecting shells, I hear people's great fat feet crunching them up far faster than I can collect them; and the ones that are left, the sea breaks up. I would not dream of collecting shells with living creatures in them or diving for them, but once their occupants have left, why should I not collect them?' If one bases this argument on the amount of luggage that can be carried home by one man, the sum beauty of whose work is often greater than its natural parts, it becomes very convincing indeed.

line 71

1 What does the reader learn about Peter Cooke in the first paragraph?

  A He has produced hand-made objects in different materials.
  B He was praised for his shell objects many years ago.
  C He hopes to work with other materials in the future.
  D He has written about his love of making shell objects.

2 When looking round his apartment, the writer

  A is attracted by Cooke's personality.
  B senses that Cooke wants his products to be admired.
  C realises he finds Cooke's work boring.
  D feels uncertain about giving Cooke his opinion.

3 The 'small sacrifice' in line 25 refers to

  A the loss of Cooke's ornaments.
  B the display of Cooke's ornaments.
  C the cost of keeping Cooke's ornaments.
  D the space required to store Cooke's ornaments.

4 When the writer enquires about the cost of his shell objects, Cooke

  A cleverly changes the subject.
  B defends the prices charged for his work.
  C says he has no idea why the level is so high.
  D notes that his work will not always be so popular.

5 What does Cooke regret about his work?

  A He is not as famous as he should have been.
  B He makes less money than he should make.
  C He is less imaginative than he used to be.
  D He is not as skilful as he used to be.

6 When talking about the artist's working method, the writer suspects that Cooke

  A accepts that he sometimes makes mistakes.
  B is unaware of the unique quality his work has.
  C underrates his creative contribution.
  D undervalues the materials that he uses.

7 What does the reader learn about Cooke's shell-collecting activities?

  A Not everyone approves of what he does.
  B Other methods might make his work easier.
  C Other tourists get in the way of his collecting.
  D Not all shells are the right size and shape for his work.

8 What does 'it' in line 71 refer to?

  A Cooke's luggage
  B Cooke's argument
  C the beauty of Cooke's work
  D the reason for Cooke's trips

Part 2

You are going to read a magazine article about a new hotel. Seven sentences have been removed from the article. Choose from the sentences **A–H** the one which fits each gap (**9–15**). There is one extra sentence which you do not need to use.

Mark your answers **on the separate answer sheet**.

Five-star luxury meets up-to-date technology

The five-star Merrion Hotel, which has just opened, is the result of considerable research into customer requirements and nearly two years' work converting four large eighteenth-century houses in Dublin. Creating a new hotel in this way has allowed the latest technology to be installed. This has been done for the benefit of staff and guests alike.

At the Merrion, General Manager Peter MacCann expects his staff to know the guests by name. **9** It can deal with return clients in the extra-special way that is appropriate to a five-star hotel.

Though the system cost £250,000 to install, it will pay for itself over time, according to MacCann. **10** For example, a guest who requests certain music CDs during a first stay will find those same CDs ready for him on a return visit. This is thanks to the guest-history facility which allows staff to key in any number of preferences.

Hotel guests the world over frequently complain about room temperature. **11** Guests have the opportunity to change the temperature themselves within three degrees either side of the normal 18°C but, in addition, each individual room can be adjusted by any amount between 14°C and 25°C at the front desk.

12 This is particularly true for the business user, and MacCann estimates that up to sixty-five per cent of his business will come from this part of the market. To provide the best service for such needs, the hotel has taken the traditional business centre and put it into individual bedrooms. Each one has three phones, two phone lines, a fax machine that doubles as a photocopier and printer, and a video-conferencing facility.

Technology changes so quickly these days that the hotel has had to try to forecast possible improvements. **13** The televisions are rented rather than bought, so that they can be replaced with more up-to-date models at any time. DVD recorders can also be upgraded when necessary.

Despite the presence of all this very up-to-the-minute equipment in the rooms, MacCann says they have tried hard not to make guests feel threatened by the technology. **14** There are, of course, a swimming pool and gym, six conference rooms, two bars and two restaurants, and a beautiful garden at the heart of it all.

As at all luxury hotels, the food that is offered to guests must be excellent. Chef Patrick Guilbaud's Dublin restaurant already had two Michelin stars when he agreed to move his restaurant business to the Merrion. **15** He has been able to design a new kitchen and take it into the modern age. There are better parking facilities than at the previous address, too. From the hotel's side, they are able to offer a popular and successful place to eat, with no financial risks attached.

Aided by technology and a highly capable staff, the Merrion looks likely to succeed.

A For guests, though, it is the other technology offered in their rooms which is most likely to find favour.

B Being part of the hotel site has huge benefits, both for him and the hotel itself.

C Extra cables have been laid to handle whatever scientific advances may occur.

D He expects fifty per cent of the rooms to be occupied in the hotel's first year.

E Another hi-tech system controls this essential area of comfort.

F However, for details of his guests' preferences, he relies on the hotel's computer system.

G The one hundred and forty-five bedrooms, large and well-furnished, are both comfortable and welcoming.

H He praises its efficiency and talks enthusiastically of the facilities it offers.

Part 3

You are going to read a magazine article about members of a part-time drama club called The Globe Players. For questions **16–30**, choose from the people (**A–F**). The people may be chosen more than once. When more than one answer is required, these may be given in any order.

Mark your answers **on the separate answer sheet**.

Which person or people

mentions joining because of loneliness?	16
had some theatre experience before joining The Globe Players?	17
has a high opinion of The Globe Players?	18
joined to keep busy?	19
has mixed feelings about finishing a show?	20
have difficulty finding suitable roles?	21 22
enjoys being with people who have different ideas?	23
thinks that acting is out of character for them?	24
mentions the publicity they sometimes receive?	25
believes the other members are like them in character?	26
talks about the complications of putting on a play?	27
feel that not everyone approves of them acting?	28 29
doubts their ability to perform?	30

The Globe Players

A Christina Howard

When I moved to this area the children were quite little, and I wondered how I was ever going to meet people. Then I met Susanna Dickster, who was the organiser of The Globe Players, and she said, 'Do you want to join?' And I said, 'Well, yes, all right.' They appeared to be incredibly extrovert people, which I suppose I am by nature too. For three years I was the theatre manager. I think I make a better manager than an actress, but I did have a dream role in a play the year before last.

B Eric Plumber

I do about one play a year, just out of interest. But I'm a quiet sort of chap, not one of the world's extroverts, and yet here I am in an extrovert field, doing theatrical activities. There is a sort of magic to the theatre. There's a sense of togetherness with the rest of the actors in the cast. When a play is over, on the last night, there's a combination of anticlimax and relief. It's rather nice to think you will be able to do all the things that you weren't able to do when the play was on. But there's also a sense of loss, so you look forward to the next play.

C Laura Goldcrest

I have done some stage management for productions at my school and when I saw the play The Globe Players were going to do next, I thought I'd try for it. Usually there are not a lot of parts for people my age, so when there was this opportunity, I went along and auditioned. It went all right, and I got the part. Lots of my friends just hang around with people of their own age, but there are people at The Globe Players who are quite old, and I get talking to them about all sorts of things. It's amazing how our views differ, but we have lovely conversations.

D Clare MacDonald

When I was at school, I used to think I'd rather like to go on stage. But then other things came along. One job I did was as a stewardess for an airline. That's like giving a performance. I left the airline and joined The Globe Players. My husband will always come to performances, but he does tend to moan a bit because he feels it takes up too much time. As a club I feel we are very professional. I do about one play a year, which is quite enough for me. Obviously, there are fewer parts as you get older, particularly for women: one can no longer play Juliet or other young parts, which I feel sad about.

E Robin Wilson

I work behind the scenes with The Globe Players because it's always a challenge. For instance, the last play I did needed a full-sized, working swimming pool. Well, most amateur theatres have a bucket of water in the wings. But our director said, 'I want a real swimming pool on that set. Go away and do it.' It was a real challenge for me. However, we did it. We got more reviews than we usually do because, of course, it was something different. And quite a lot of amateur societies came to see if they could do it – and a lot of them decided they couldn't.

F Mike James

I was a science teacher and took early retirement from my college. After twenty-four years it was a bit hard and I got rather bored. During that time it was good to have the drama group. It takes your mind off things; you can't act and worry about something else. But it's very disruptive to a family – my wife will tell you that. Teaching in a way is like being on stage. When you go into a class you may not be feeling very well, you are not necessarily very keen on the subject you are teaching – the whole thing adds up to a no-no. But you go in, you are enthusiastic and you try to generate interest, and it's an act.

PAPER 2   WRITING (1 hour 20 minutes)

Part 1

You **must** answer this question. Write your answer in **120–150** words in an appropriate style.

---

1   You are studying in Britain and you have recently received a letter from an English friend, Kate, who is interested in arranging a day trip for a group of students. Read Kate's letter, the advertisement and the notes you have made. Then write a letter to Kate, using **all** your notes.

> . . . *and the students in my class are really interested in going on a day trip. I know you went on a boat trip with your English class recently. Could you tell me what it was like and whether you'd recommend it?*
>
> *Kate*

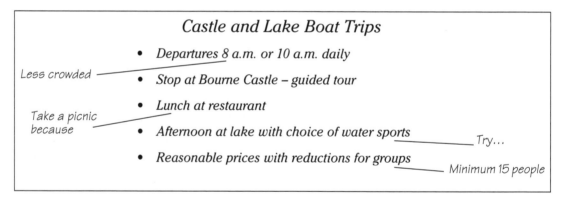

Castle and Lake Boat Trips

Less crowded —

- *Departures 8 a.m. or 10 a.m. daily*
- *Stop at Bourne Castle – guided tour*
- *Lunch at restaurant*

Take a picnic because

- *Afternoon at lake with choice of water sports* ———— *Try...*
- *Reasonable prices with reductions for groups* ———— *Minimum 15 people*

Write your **letter**. You must use grammatically correct sentences with accurate spelling and punctuation in a style appropriate for the situation.

Do not write any postal addresses.

Part 2

Write an answer to **one** of the questions **2–5** in this part. Write your answer in **120–180** words in an appropriate style.

2 An English language club is starting in your area. The organisers of the club have asked you to write a report giving your suggestions about:

- how often the club should meet
- what type of activities it should organise
- how the club could be advertised.

Write your **report**.

3 You have decided to enter a short story competition in an international magazine. The competition rules say that the story must **begin** with the following words.

It was three o'clock in the morning when the phone rang.

Write your **story**.

4 You have seen this announcement in *Leisure and Entertainment* magazine.

Could you live without television for a week?

Write and tell us what difference this would make to your life.

We will publish the best article.

Write your **article**.

5 Answer **one** of the following two questions based on **one** of the titles below.

(a) *Officially Dead* – Richard Prescott

You have had a class discussion about the relationship between Mark and Julie in *Officially Dead*. Your teacher has now given you this essay for homework.

In which ways does Mark help Julie?

Write your **essay**.

(b) *Pride and Prejudice* – Jane Austen

You see this notice in your college magazine.

Unpleasant Characters! – Articles wanted.

Have you read a book recently with characters you really disliked? Tell us about them!

Write your **article** about two characters you disliked in *Pride and Prejudice*, giving your reasons.

PAPER 3   USE OF ENGLISH (45 minutes)

Part 1

For questions **1–12**, read the text below and decide which answer (**A**, **B**, **C** or **D**) best fits each gap. There is an example at the beginning (**0**).

Mark your answers **on the separate answer sheet**.

Example:

0   **A** planet   **B** world   **C** earth   **D** globe

0	A	B	C	D
	—	▬	—	—

Markets

In practically any country in the **(0)** ..... , you are **(1)** ..... to find a market somewhere. Markets have been with us since **(2)** ..... times, and arose wherever people needed to exchange the goods they produced. For example, a farmer might have exchanged a cow for tools. But just as times have **(3)** ..... , so have market practices. So, **(4)** ..... in early times the main activity **(5)** ..... with markets would have been 'bartering' – in **(6)** ..... words exchanging goods – today most stall-holders wouldn't be too **(7)** ..... on accepting potatoes as payment, for instance, instead of cash.

In contrast, what might be a common **(8)** ..... in a modern market in some countries is a certain amount of 'haggling', where customer and seller eventually **(9)** ..... on a price, after what can sometimes be quite a heated debate. However, behaviour which is **(10)** ..... in a market in one country may not be acceptable in another. Even within one country, there may be some markets where you could haggle quite **(11)** ..... and others where it would be **(12)** ..... not to try!

1   **A** inevitable   **B** confident   **C** definite   **D** sure

2   **A** ancient   **B** antique   **C** old   **D** past

3   **A** changed   **B** turned   **C** developed   **D** differed

4   **A** however   **B** despite   **C** nevertheless   **D** whereas

5   **A** associated   **B** relating   **C** connecting   **D** attached

6   **A** different   **B** other   **C** new   **D** alternative

7   **A** fond   **B** keen   **C** eager   **D** pleased

8   **A** look   **B** vision   **C** sight   **D** view

9   **A** confirm   **B** consent   **C** approve   **D** agree

10 **A** expected   **B** insisted   **C** believed   **D** reckoned

11 **A** simply   **B** plainly   **C** clearly   **D** easily

12 **A** profitable   **B** advisable   **C** noticeable   **D** acceptable

Part 2

For questions **13–24**, read the text below and think of the word which best fits each gap. Use only **one** word in each gap. There is an example at the beginning (**0**).

Write your answers **IN CAPITAL LETTERS on the separate answer sheet**.

Example:

0	H	I	S														

Charles Dickens' childhood experiences

Charles Dickens was one of the greatest nineteenth-century English novelists. At the time of **(0)** ...*his*.... death in 1870 he was a wealthy man, in contrast to the poverty of his early days. His parents **(13)** .*did*. their best to look after him but were always in difficulties **(14)** .*with*. money. Eventually, his father owed **(15)** .*quite* a large amount of money that he was sent to prison for three months.

Two days after his twelfth birthday, Dickens was taken away from school by his parents and made **(16)** .*him*.. work in a factory to increase the family income. Factories could be dangerous places in **(17)** .*those* days and some employers were cruel. Charles was not **(18)** .*that*. extremely unhappy, but also ashamed of working there, and he **(19)** .*would* never forget that period of his life. In his novels Dickens showed just how shocking working and living conditions were.

Working in the factory affected him so deeply that he found **(20)** .*sometimes*... much too painful to speak about in later life. His own wife and children knew **(21)** .*nothing* at all about the unhappiness of his childhood while Dickens was still alive, **(22)** .*but*... shortly after his death a biography was published in **(23)** ..*the*.. Dickens' terrible childhood experiences in the factory were revealed **(24)** ..*for*... the first time.

Part 3

For questions **25–34**, read the text below. Use the word given in capitals at the end of some of the lines to form a word that fits in the gap **in the same line**. There is an example at the beginning (**0**).

Write your answers **IN CAPITAL LETTERS on the separate answer sheet**.

Example: | 0 | E | X | T | R | E | M | E | L | Y | | | | | | | |

The London Underground map

Many people would agree that the London Underground map is

(0) ....*extremely*.... well designed. It is not only simple and easy to understand   **EXTREME**

but also quite (25) ...*attractive*... and, most importantly, it performs its primary   **ATTRACT**

task of guiding both Londoners and (26) ...*touring*... round the Underground   **TOUR**

system in the city very well. The man behind this great (27) ...*achievement*... was   **ACHIEVE**

called Henry Beck. He was an (28) ...*employee*... of the London Underground   **EMPLOY**

Drawing Office, and first came up with his design for the map in 1931.

The map which had been in use before 1931 was messy and (29) ...*unclear.*... .   **CLEAR**

Beck decided that a (30) ...*traditional*... map, which gives accurate information   **TRADITION**

about distance, was not necessary for the Underground and instead

produced a diagram which showed only the stations on the Underground

system. This new map was an enormous (31) ...*success*... with the public   **SUCCEED**

when, in 1933, it made its first (32) ...*appearing*... on Underground platforms   **APPEAR**

and at station entrances.

The design of the map showed great (33) ...*oregin*... because it provided   **ORIGINAL**

a very clear representation of a highly complex network of (34) ...*communication*... .   **COMMUNICATE**

Beck's approach was later adopted by most of the world's underground

systems.

Part 4

For questions **35–42**, complete the second sentence so that it has a similar meaning to the first sentence, using the word given. **Do not change the word given**. You must use between **two** and **five** words, including the word given. Here is an example (**0**).

Example:

0   You must do exactly what the manager tells you.

   CARRY

   You must .... instructions exactly.

The gap can be filled by the words 'carry out the manager's', so you write:

Example:	0	CARRY OUT THE MANAGER'S

Write **only** the missing words **IN CAPITAL LETTERS on the separate answer sheet**.

---

35   While I was on holiday, a lot of interesting things happened to me.

   MY

   During ...*my holiday I had*........ a lot of interesting experiences.

36   It was careless of you to leave without locking the door.

   OUGHT

   You ...*ought to lock*..................... the door before you left.

37   'Is Pete likely to change his mind?' Rob asked.

   CHANCE

   'Is there ...*any change of pete* *might*...... changing his mind?' Rob asked.

38   Paul is the only person who has replied to the invitation.

   NOBODY

   Apart ...*from Paul nobody* *had*......... replied to the invitation.

39 Are you familiar with his teaching style yet?

USED

Have you ...*got used to*............ his teaching style yet?

40 It was such a sunny day that none of us wanted to do any work.

FELT

None of us ....*felt like doing*......... any work because it was such a sunny day.

41 Barbara couldn't sing or dance.

UNABLE

Besides ...*from unable to sing*...., Barbara couldn't dance either.

42 Dinner will be served immediately upon our arrival at the hotel.

SOON

Dinner will be served ...*soon after our arrival*................. at the hotel.

PAPER 4   LISTENING (approximately 40 minutes)

Part 1

You will hear people talking in eight different situations. For questions **1–8**, choose the best answer (**A**, **B** or **C**).

1   You overhear a man talking about an experience he had at an airport.
    What did he lose?

   A   his passport

   B   his wallet

   C   a piece of luggage

2   You hear an advertisement on the radio.
    What is special about the *Fretlight* guitar?

   A   It plays recorded music.

   B   It teaches you how to play.

   C   It plugs into a computer.

3   You hear part of a radio programme.
    What is the presenter talking about?

   A   food safety

   B   meal times

   C   healthy recipes

4   You hear two people discussing a type of pollution.
    What do the speakers agree about?

   A   the best way to solve the problem

   B   how they feel about this type of pollution

   C   how they reacted to the solution they saw

5 You hear a conversation between a shop assistant and a customer about a compact disc.
What was the cause of the problem?

    A   The customer gave the wrong number.

    B   A mistake was made on the order form.

    C   The disc was incorrectly labelled.

6 You overhear a conversation at a football game.
What does the speaker say about his team?

    A   They're better than usual.

    B   They're as good as he expected.

    C   They tend to be unlucky.

7 You overhear a schoolgirl talking to her friend.
What does she think about her new teacher?

    A   He is clever.

    B   He is funny.

    C   He is interesting.

8 In a hotel you overhear a conversation.
Who is the woman?

    A   a tour guide

    B   a tourist

    C   a hotel receptionist

Part 2

You will hear part of a radio interview with a swimming instructor. For questions **9–18**, complete the sentences.

Swimming instructor

Paul works at a hotel in the [_____ **9**]

He started his job in [_____ **10**]

He particularly likes meeting [_____ **11**] there.

Paul isn't interested in teaching [_____ **12**]

According to Paul, [_____ **13**] of all adults can't swim.

Paul's students are afraid of going [_____ **14**]

His students have to put their faces into a salad bowl and

[_____ **15**] below the surface.

The first thing they do in the pool is to [_____ **16**]

in the water with their faces down.

Paul thinks it's essential to be [_____ **17**] in the water.

Most people learn to swim after about [_____ **18**]

Part 3

You will hear part of a radio programme called *Morning Market*. Five listeners have telephoned the programme because they have something to sell. For questions **19–23**, choose which of the statements (**A–F**) matches the reason each of the people gives for selling their possession. Use the letters only once. There is one extra letter which you do not need to use.

A I didn't enjoy using it.

Speaker 1 | 19 |

B I made a mistake.

Speaker 2 | 20 |

C It's an unwanted prize.

Speaker 3 | 21 |

D It takes up too much space.

Speaker 4 | 22 |

E I've got something better.

Speaker 5 | 23 |

F I have health problems.

Part 4

You will hear an interview with a man who makes models for films and television. For questions **24–30**, choose the best answer (**A**, **B** or **C**).

---

24 Matt got a job doing holiday relief work because he wanted

    A   to do part-time work.

    B   a career in photography.

    C   to work in television.

25 What did Matt find 'interesting' about the sixties?

    A   the fascination with space travel

    B   the increased number of comic books

    C   the advances in photography

26 Why were Matt's models used on the news?

    A   They were better than pictures.

    B   Some equipment had been destroyed.

    C   The studio was trying new ideas.

27 Matt thinks he was successful at getting work in television because

    A   he had good experience.

    B   he knew some of the staff.

    C   he was available at the right time.

28 Matt worked on *Bright Star* as

    A   part of a team.

    B   the producer.

    C   a design student.

29 Matt was invited on children's television to

    A   tell stories about his design work.

    B   explain the purpose of space research.

    C   help children make models themselves.

30 Matt remembers *Heart of Darkness* because

    A   it was his favourite comedy.

    B   his work was recognised.

    C   a film was made of it.

PAPER 5 SPEAKING (14 minutes)

You take the Speaking test with another candidate, referred to here as your partner. There are two examiners. One will speak to you and your partner and the other will be listening. Both examiners will award marks.

Part 1 (3 minutes)

The examiner asks you and your partner questions about yourselves. You may be asked about things like 'your home town', 'your interests', 'your career plans', etc.

Part 2 (a one-minute 'long turn' for each candidate, plus 20-second response from the second candidate)

The examiner gives you two photographs and asks you to talk about them for one minute. The examiner then asks your partner a question about your photographs and your partner responds briefly.

Then the examiner gives your partner two different photographs. Your partner talks about these photographs for one minute. This time the examiner asks you a question about your partner's photographs and you respond briefly.

Part 3 (approximately 3 minutes)

The examiner asks you and your partner to talk together. You may be asked to solve a problem or try to come to a decision about something. For example, you might be asked to decide the best way to use some rooms in a language school. The examiner gives you a picture to help you but does not join in the conversation.

Part 4 (approximately 4 minutes)

The interlocutor asks some further questions, which leads to a more general discussion of what you have talked about in Part 3. You may comment on your partner's answers if you wish.

Visual materials for the Speaking test

1A

1B

1E

1C

1D

2A

2B

2E

2C

2D

3A

3B

3E

3C

3D

4A

4B

4E

4C

4D

Test 4

PAPER 1   READING (1 hour)

Part 1

You are going to read an article in which a film critic talks about his work. For questions **1–8**, choose the answer (**A**, **B**, **C** or **D**) which you think fits best according to the text.

Mark your answers **on the separate answer sheet**.

Film Critic

Mark Adams looks back over the last ten years of his work
as a film critic for a newspaper called *The Front Page*.

Writing articles about films for *The Front Page* was my first proper job. Before then I had done bits of reviewing – novels for other newspapers, films for a magazine and anything I was asked to do for the radio. That was how I met Tom Seaton, the first arts editor of *The Front Page*, who had also written for radio and television. He hired me, but Tom was not primarily a journalist, or he would certainly have been more careful in choosing his staff.

At first, his idea was that a team of critics should take care of the art forms that didn't require specialised knowledge: books, TV, theatre, film and radio. There would be a weekly lunch at which we would make our choices from the artistic material that Tom had decided we should cover, though there would also be guests to make the atmosphere sociable.

It all felt like a bit of a dream at that time: a new newspaper, and I was one of the team. It seemed so unlikely that a paper could be introduced into a crowded market. It seemed just as likely that a millionaire wanted to help me personally, and was pretending to employ me. Such was my lack of self-confidence. In fact, the first time I saw someone reading the newspaper on the London Underground, then turning to a page on which one of my reviews appeared, I didn't know where to look.

Tom's original scheme for a team of critics for the arts never took off. It was a good idea, but we *line 31* didn't get together as planned and so everything was done by phone. It turned out, too, that the general public out there preferred to associate a reviewer with a single subject area, and so I chose film. Without Tom's initial push, though, we would hardly have come up with the present arrangement, by which I write an extended weekly piece, usually on one film.

The luxury of this way of working suits me *line 40* well. I wouldn't have been interested in the more standard film critic's role, which involves considering every film that comes out. That's a routine that would make me stale in no time at all. I would soon be sinking into my seat on a Monday morning with the sigh, 'What insulting rubbish must I sit through now?' – a style of sigh that can often be heard in screening rooms around the world.

The space I am given allows me to broaden my argument – or forces me, in an uninteresting week, to make something out of nothing. But what is my role in the public arena? I assume that people choose what films to go to on the basis of the stars, the publicity or the director. There is also such a thing as loyalty to 'type' or its opposite. It can only rarely happen that someone who hates westerns buys a ticket for one after reading a review, or a love story addict avoids a romantic film because of what the papers say.

So if a film review isn't really a consumer guide, what is it? I certainly don't feel I have a responsibility to be 'right' about a movie. Nor do I think there should be a certain number of 'great' and 'bad' films each year. All I have to do is put forward an argument. I'm not a judge, and nor would I want to be.

1   What do we learn about Tom Seaton in the first paragraph?

  A   He encouraged Mark to become a writer.
  B   He has worked in various areas of the media.
  C   He met Mark when working for television.
  D   He prefers to employ people that he knows.

2   The weekly lunches were planned in order to

  A   help the writers get to know each other.
  B   provide an informal information session.
  C   distribute the work that had to be done.
  D   entertain important visitors from the arts.

3   When Mark first started working for *The Front Page*, he

  A   doubted the paper would succeed.
  B   was embarrassed at being recognised.
  C   felt it needed some improvement.
  D   was surprised to be earning so much.

4   What does Mark mean when he says that Tom's scheme 'never took off' (line 31)?

  A   It was unpopular.
  B   It wasted too much time.
  C   It wasn't planned properly.
  D   It wasn't put into practice.

5   In the end, the organisation of the team was influenced by

  A   readers' opinions.
  B   the availability of writers.
  C   pressure of time.
  D   the popularity of subjects.

6   Why does Mark refer to his way of working as a 'luxury' (line 40)?

  A   He can please more readers.
  B   He is able to make choices.
  C   His working hours are flexible.
  D   He is able to see a lot of films.

7   In Mark's opinion, his articles

  A   are seldom read by filmgoers.
  B   are ignored by stars and film directors.
  C   have little effect on public viewing habits.
  D   are more persuasive than people realise.

8   Which of the following best describes what Mark says about his work?

  A   His success varies from year to year.
  B   He prefers to write about films he likes.
  C   He can freely express his opinion.
  D   He writes according to accepted rules.

Part 2

You are going to read a newspaper article about a dentist. Seven sentences have been removed from the article. Choose from the sentences **A–H** the one which fits each gap (**9–15**). There is one extra sentence which you do not need to use.

Mark your answers **on the separate answer sheet.**

Fun at the Dentist's?

If you walk into W. Lloyd Jerome's dental surgery in the centre of Glasgow, you'll see bright modern paintings on the wall and a fashionable blue couch which patients sit on while he checks their teeth. Jerome says, 'Fifty per cent of the population only go to the dentist when they're in pain rather than attending for regular check-ups. That's because they're frightened.'

To counteract this, he has tried to create an environment where people are not afraid. ' **9** ' I find that's one of the things that people associate with pain. In fact, my philosophy is that dental treatment should take place in an atmosphere of relaxation, interest and above all enjoyment.'

Which is all highly shocking for anyone (most of us in fact) who has learnt to associate dental treatment with pain, or at the very least, with formal, clinical visits. Jerome says, ' **10** '

Virtual-reality headsets are one of his new relaxation techniques. ' **11** The headsets are used for the initial check-up, where the patient sits comfortably on the blue couch and watches a film about underwater wildlife while I look at their teeth. Then the headset switches to a special camera, to give the patient a visual tour around their mouth.' Surprisingly, most patients seem to enjoy this part of their visit to the dentist.

Another key point is that the surgery smells more like a perfume shop than a dentist's. Today there is the smell of orange. Jerome explains, ' **12** Smell is very important. That dental smell of surgical spirit can get the heart racing in minutes if you're frightened of dentists.' I certainly found the delicate smell in the surgery very pleasant.

Although he is known as Glasgow's most fashionable dentist, Jerome is keen to point out that he takes his work very seriously. ' **13** '

For example, Jerome uses a special instrument which sprays warm water on the teeth to clean them, rather than scraping them. ' **14** '

Five years ago, Jerome went to the United States to do research into dental techniques. ' **15** ', he explains. He sees his patient-centred attitude as the start of a gradual movement towards less formality in the conservative British dentistry profession.

At that moment, a patient arrives. Jerome rushes over, offers him a cup of tea (herbal or regular), asks him what video he'd like to watch and leads him gently towards the chair. The patient seems to be enjoying this five-star treatment and no wonder. The surgery seems more like an elegant beauty parlour than a mainstream dental practice.

A One of the things I found out there was that when you make it easier for the patient you make it easier for yourself.

B That's why I took the decision not to wear a white coat.

C If people are relaxed, entertained and correctly treated, they will forget such previous negative experiences.

D The relaxation techniques are important but the quality of the treatment is of course the most important thing.

E We were the first practice in Britain to introduce them and they're proving very popular.

F It feels a bit strange at first, but as long as people are relaxed, it's not painful at all.

G Now I'm sure that they actually look forward to their visits here.

H When people walk in, I want them to realise with all their senses that it's not like going to the dentist's.

Part 3

You are going to read a magazine article about theme parks in Britain. For questions **16–30**, choose from the theme parks (**A–E**). The theme parks may be chosen more than once.

Mark your answers **on the separate answer sheet.**

Of which theme parks are the following stated?

We had no previous experience of places like this.	16
Some of the children showed they were frightened on a certain ride.	17
The children were all young enough to enjoy it.	18
It was good that you could find somewhere to rest.	19
It was more enjoyable than we had expected.	20
The children disagreed about what was the most frightening ride.	21
The surroundings are not particularly attractive.	22
We didn't mind having to wait to go on the rides.	23
The children wanted to stay longer than we did.	24
One of the rides seemed to finish very quickly.	25
We were glad that the children couldn't go on a certain ride.	26
One of the children had a better time than we had expected.	27
It makes a claim which is accurate.	28
None of the rides would frighten young children very much.	29
The manner of some employees seemed rather unfriendly.	30

Variations on a Theme

If you're thinking of taking children to a theme park, there are dozens to choose from in Britain. We asked five families to test the best.

A Fun Island – The Burns family

Last year we went to a huge theme park in the US and we thought that Fun Island might seem dull by comparison. In fact, we were impressed. The park tries hard to cater for younger children, so our three-year-old didn't feel left out. The kids all loved the Crocodile Ride and the Giant Wheel. There's a special dodgems ride for the very young kids, which was a great success. For older children, there are scarier rides, such as Splash Out, where you end up jumping in a pool! After five hours, Steve and I were ready to call it a day, but the children objected because they were having such fun. Our only criticism would be that the park is slightly lacking in atmosphere, and the scenery leaves something to be desired. But the staff are extremely helpful and we felt it was clean, well organised and very security-conscious.

B Wonderland – The McMillan family

None of us had been to a theme park before, so we didn't know what to expect. We thought Oscar might be too young, but he adored it. He was in heaven on the Mountain Train, and particularly liked Little Land, with its small replicas of famous buildings that were at his level! The older children enjoyed the ferris wheel, and loved driving the toy cars on a proper road layout. We spent six hours there and were glad that there were places where you could put your feet up. The landscaping is perfect and the staff very helpful and friendly. And there's something for everyone, adults included.

C Adventure World – The Jeffree family

After seven hours we felt there was still a lot to see. The children loved the Big Top Circus, which had a fantastic trapeze act and kept us on the edge of our seats. We went on the Terror Line and, although the girls were rather scared and kept their eyes shut most of the time, they said they'd enjoyed it. Their favourite ride was Running River, where you think you're going to get soaked, but you don't. For younger children, Toy Land is great fun. The children had a look at the new ride, Fear Factor, but we breathed a sigh of relief when they found that they were too small to go on it! The park is so well designed that even queuing for rides isn't too boring. It's spotlessly clean, and the staff are great. On one ride I couldn't sit with both girls, so a member of staff offered to go with one of them.

D The Great Park – The Langridge family

We arrived at one o'clock and were disappointed that the park was only open until 5 p.m. This is a super theme park for younger children because the rides aren't too terrifying. I'm a real coward but even I enjoyed myself. We all adored Exotic Travels, a boat ride which starts off quite tamely and then becomes terrific fun. We queued for half an hour for Lightning River, and then it was over before we knew it! I wouldn't go on the Big Leap, but if you have the nerve, it looked great. If the children had been a little older, they might have found it a bit tame, but they were all in the right age group and they loved it.

E Fantasy World – The Breakall family

According to the park's advertising there is 'No Limit to the Fun', and we certainly felt that was true. Europe's tallest roller-coaster, the Rocket, dominates the skyline, and Ben thought it was the most terrifying of the rides, although Jennie said the Hanger, where you hang upside-down 30 metres above the ground, was even worse! There are a dozen or so main rides, which the older children went on several times. Sarah was too small for a couple of them, but enjoyed the Long Slide. We found the staff attitudes were mixed. Some of them were great with the younger children, but the welcome wasn't always as warm. You need a full day to enjoy Fantasy World. We wouldn't have dared tell the kids we were going home early.

PAPER 2 WRITING (1 hour 20 minutes)

Part 1

You **must** answer this question. Write your answer in **120–150** words in an appropriate style.

---

1 You have received this letter from your English-speaking friend, Alex. Read the letter and the notes you have made. Then write a letter to Alex, using **all** your notes.

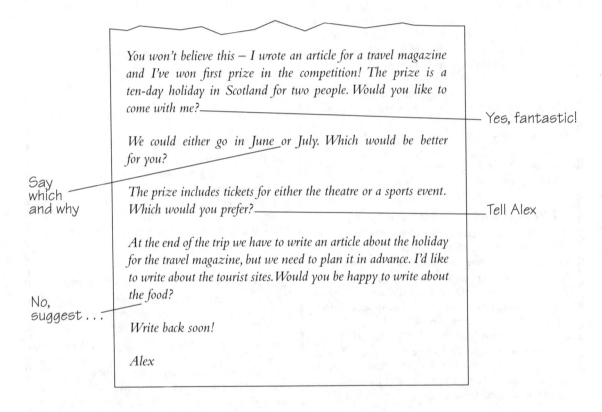

You won't believe this – I wrote an article for a travel magazine and I've won first prize in the competition! The prize is a ten-day holiday in Scotland for two people. Would you like to come with me? —————————— Yes, fantastic!

We could either go in June or July. Which would be better for you?

Say which and why

The prize includes tickets for either the theatre or a sports event. Which would you prefer? —————————— Tell Alex

At the end of the trip we have to write an article about the holiday for the travel magazine, but we need to plan it in advance. I'd like to write about the tourist sites. Would you be happy to write about the food?

No, suggest . . .

Write back soon!

Alex

Write your **letter**. You must use grammatically correct sentences with accurate spelling and punctuation in a style appropriate for the situation.

Do not write any postal addresses.

Part 2

Write an answer to **one** of the questions **2–5** in this part. Write your answer in **120–180** words in an appropriate style.

2 After a class discussion on the media's treatment of famous people, your teacher has asked you to write an essay, giving your opinions on the following statement:

> *Famous people, such as politicians and film stars, deserve to have a private life without journalists following them all the time.*

Write your **essay**.

3 You see this announcement in an international magazine.

> We invite you, our readers, to write an article on:
> **The Home of the Future**
> In what ways do you think people's homes will be
> different in the future?
> In what ways will they still be the same?
> The writer of the best article will win a prize.

Write your **article**.

4 Your English teacher has asked you to write a story for the college magazine. Your story must **begin** with the following words:

> *It was dangerous, but I knew I had to do it.*

Write your **story**.

5 Answer **one** of the following two questions based on **one** of the titles below.

(a) *Officially Dead* – Richard Prescott

You have had a class discussion about what happens to Julie in *Officially Dead*. Now your English teacher has given you this essay for homework.

How does Julie's life change after her husband's death?

Write your **essay**.

(b) *Pride and Prejudice* – Jane Austen

You have received this letter from your English friend, Kate.

```
I've recently read the book and seen the film of Pride and Prejudice.
It's a very old-fashioned story - why do you think it is still so popular
with people today?
Write soon, Kate
```

Write your **letter**.

PAPER 3   USE OF ENGLISH (45 minutes)

Part 1

For questions **1–12**, read the text below and decide which answer (**A, B, C** or **D**) best fits each gap. There is an example at the beginning (**0**).

Mark your answers **on the separate answer sheet**.

Example:

0   **A** recommended   **B** reminded   **C** recognised   **D** remembered

0	A	B	C	D
	—	—	—	▬

Famous explorer

Captain James Cook is **(0)** ..... today for being one of Britain's most famous explorers of the 18th century. Cook was **(1)** ..... most other explorers of the same period as he did not come from a wealthy family and had to work hard to **(2)** ..... his position in life. He was lucky to be **(3)** ..... by his father's employer, who saw that he was a bright boy and paid for him to attend the village school. At sixteen, he started **(4)** ..... in a shop in a fishing village, and this was a turning **(5)** ..... in his life. He developed an interest in the sea and eventually joined the Royal Navy in order to see more of the world.

Cook was **(6)** ..... by sailing, astronomy and the production of maps, and quickly became an expert in these subjects. He was also one of the first people to **(7)** ..... that scurvy, an illness often suffered by sailors, could be prevented by careful **(8)** ..... to diet. It was during his **(9)** ..... to the Pacific Ocean that Cook made his historic landing in Australia and the **(10)** ..... discovery that New Zealand was two **(11)** ..... islands. He became a national hero and still **(12)** ..... one today.

1   **A** different   **B** contrary   **C** distinct   **D** unlike (circled)

2   **A** manage (circled)   **B** succeed   **C** achieve   **D** fulfil

3   **A** remarked   **B** viewed   **C** glanced   **D** noticed (circled)

4   **A** trade   **B** work (circled)   **C** career   **D** job

5   **A** moment   **B** instant   **C** point (circled)   **D** mark

6   **A** keen   **B** eager   **C** fascinated (circled) **D** enthusiastic

7   **A** regard   **B** estimate   **C** catch   **D** realise (circled)

8   **A** attention   **B** organisation   **C** observation (circled) **D** selection

9   **A** travel (circled)   **B** voyage   **C** excursion   **D** tour

10 **A** serious   **B** superior   **C** major (circled)   **D** leading

11 **A** shared   **B** particular   **C** common   **D** separate (circled)

12 **A** remains   **B** stands (circled) **C** maintains   **D** keeps

Part 2

For questions **13–24**, read the text below and think of the word which best fits each gap. Use only **one** word in each gap. There is an example at the beginning (**0**).

Write your answers **IN CAPITAL LETTERS on the separate answer sheet**.

Example: | **0** | *M* | *O* | *S* | *T* | | | | | | | | | | | | | |

The Inferno ski race

The Inferno is the oldest and (**0**) ...*most*... celebrated of all amateur ski races. It is held every January, near Mürren in Switzerland. Anyone can take part, as (**13**) *long*. as they belong to a ski racing club.

The Inferno was the invention of a British businessman called Henry Lunn, who came up (**14**) *with*. the idea of the package holiday in the early 1900s and began taking groups of people to the Alps for winter sports. Henry's son, Arnold, grew very fond (**15**) *for*.. Mürren and he founded a ski club there in 1924. Four years (**16**) *later*, seventeen of the club's members took part (**17**) *in*.... the first Inferno race, from the top of the 2,970 metre Schilthorn mountain to Mürren below.

In those early days, they (**18**) *were*. to climb for six hours from the railway station in Mürren (**19**) *to*..... the start of the race. Today, racers use a cable car which (**20**) *took*. about twenty minutes. In the first race, the winning time for the fourteen-kilometre race was one hour, twelve minutes. (**21**) *These*. days it tends to be almost exactly an hour less. Although the skiers are very (**22**) *much*. faster now, some things haven't changed. The course, (**23**) *which*.. is steep and has sharp bends, remains (**24**) *us*... of the most demanding and frightening in the world.

Part 3

For questions **25–34**, read the text below. Use the word given in capitals at the end of some of the lines to form a word that fits in the gap **in the same line**. There is an example at the beginning (**0**).

Write your answers **IN CAPITAL LETTERS on the separate answer sheet**.

Example: | 0 | S | H | O | R | T | L | Y | | | | | | | | | |

Running round the world

Clive Baker will (**0**) ...*shortly*... be setting off on a 50,000 km run, hoping   **SHORT**

to add his name to the very small and select list of people who have

performed the (**25**) .... act of running all the way round the world.   **ORDINARY**

exstordinary

On the run he will experience extremes of temperature, from the

freezing

(**26**) .... Russian winter to the burning African summer. As if that is   **FREEZE**

cissistens

not bad enough, he has no back-up team for (**27**) .... and will be   **ASSIST**

running alone, carrying all his (**28**) .... on his back.   **EQUIP**

equipment.

When interviewed, however, Mr Baker suggested the real problem

would lie elsewhere. 'My biggest fear is not the physical challenge,

lonelyness

but (**29**) ....,' Mr Baker said. 'I'm as sociable as anyone and I'm very   **LONELY**

hopeful

(**30**) .... that, despite the difficulties that lie ahead, I will still be able   **HOPE**

friendly

to form many (**31**) .... on the way.'   **FRIEND**

On a trial of 2,000 km, run under the blazing (**32**) *hoting* of the African sun,   **HOT**

posoness

he came across wild baboons and (**33**) .... snakes, but such dangers   **POISON**

have not put him off. His trial run proved that a target of 60 kilometres

a day was (**34**) .... 'I have made up my mind to do it and I will.   **REASON**

Running is my life,' he said.

reasonable

Part 4

For questions **35–42**, complete the second sentence so that it has a similar meaning to the first sentence, using the word given. **Do not change the word given**. You must use between **two** and **five** words, including the word given. Here is an example (**0**).

Example:

0   You must do exactly what the manager tells you.

CARRY

You must .... instructions exactly.

The gap can be filled by the words 'carry out the manager's' so you write:

| **Example:** | **0** | *CARRY OUT THE MANAGER'S* |

Write **only** the missing words **IN CAPITAL LETTERS on the separate answer sheet**.

---

35   That's the strangest film I've ever seen!

STRANGE

I've ..*never seen such a* ~~strange~~.............. film before!

36   A very friendly taxi driver drove us into town.

DRIVEN

We ..*had driven into town* ~~with~~..... a very friendly taxi driver.

37   My aunt was determined to pay for our tickets.

INSISTED

My aunt ..*had insisted to pay*... for our tickets.

38   The manager failed to persuade Karen to take the job.

SUCCEED

The manager ..*did not succeed to* ~~persuade~~...... Karen to take the job.

39 'I'd rather you didn't use that mobile phone in here,' said the librarian.

MIND

'Would ~~you mind not to use~~ that mobile phone in here?' said the librarian.

40 John impressed his new boss by settling down to work quickly.

GOOD

John ~~had made good impression to~~ his new boss by settling down to work quickly.

41 Tony regrets lying to his teacher.

WISHES

Tony ~~wishes he had told~~ his teacher the truth.

42 I found it difficult to follow the instructions.

TROUBLE

I ~~trouble with following~~ the instructions.

PAPER 4   LISTENING (approximately 40 minutes)

Part 1

You will hear people talking in eight different situations. For questions **1–8**, choose the best answer (**A**, **B** or **C**).

1   You overhear some people talking at a party in a hotel.
    Where did the people first meet each other?

    A   at school

    B   at work

    C   at a wedding

2   You overhear a conversation in a restaurant.
    Why haven't they seen each other lately?

    A   He has been too busy.

    B   He has been ill.

    C   He has been away.

3   You overhear someone talking about a concert.
    How did she feel at the time?

    A   angry

    B   frightened

    C   disappointed

4   You hear a writer of children's stories talking about books and compact discs.
    What advantage does he think books have over compact discs?

    A   They may last for a longer time.

    B   They are easier to look after.

    C   They contain better quality material.

5 You hear a husband and wife talking about their summer holidays.
What problem do they have?

    A   They really hate flying anywhere.

    B   They can never think of anywhere to go.

    C   They never agree about what to do.

6 You hear a researcher being asked about her work.
What is she doing when she speaks?

    A   denying an accusation

    B   disproving a theory

    C   accepting a criticism

7 You overhear a woman talking to a friend on a train.
What does the woman think of the course she has attended?

    A   It has made her feel more confident.

    B   It has made her feel less confident.

    C   It hasn't made much difference to how she feels.

8 You overhear a woman speaking on the radio.
What is she doing?

    A   complaining about something

    B   apologising for something

    C   explaining something

Part 2

You will hear a radio report about dolphins. For questions **9–18**, complete the sentences.

Dolphins

Dolphins have been known to protect swimmers from sharks by getting into a

	9

Dolphins and humans have | **10** | of the same size.

Swimming with dolphins can help common problems like

	11

Some people think dolphins are able to recognise human | **12** |

Dolphins have been used to teach children to | **13** |

Swimming with dolphins is used as a | **14** |

in projects with children.

In one jaw, dolphins have as many as | **15** |

Dolphins can maintain a fast pace in the water for | **16** |

without stopping.

Dolphins make use of | **17** | to find fish.

Dolphins can be caught in | **18** | or damaged by pollution.

Part 3

You will hear five different people talking about the head teacher or principal of their former secondary school. For questions **19–23**, choose from the list (**A–F**) what each speaker is saying. Use the letters only once. There is one extra letter which you do not need to use.

A She favoured the talented students.

Speaker 1 | 19 |

B She prepared us for the real world.

Speaker 2 | 20 |

C She encouraged us to be imaginative.

Speaker 3 | 21 |

D She was ahead of her time.

Speaker 4 | 22 |

E She was concerned about the environment.

Speaker 5 | 23 |

F She encouraged competitiveness.

Part 4

You will hear an interview with a tour leader who works for an adventure company in Africa. For questions **24–30**, choose the best answer (**A**, **B** or **C**).

---

24 Don says that most of his passengers

    A   are not students.

    B   are looking for jobs.

    C   work in conservation.

25 When Don first meets a group, he

    A   gives them blankets for the overnight trip.

    B   shows them where to sit on the truck.

    C   checks they have the right equipment.

26 Don remembers one trip when

    A   he failed to take enough food.

    B   someone made a mistake with the food.

    C   someone complained about the food.

27 Don oversees the domestic work because

    A   he doesn't like to lose things.

    B   it has to be done within an hour.

    C   people complain if things are dirty.

28 If people argue, Don says that he

    A   prefers not to get involved.

    B   separates the people concerned.

    C   asks the group for a solution.

29 Don says that he sometimes

    A   needs to get to sleep early.

    B   has to camp in a noisy area.

    C   tells people when to go to bed.

30 What does Don say about getting up?

    A   He ignores any complaints about the time.

    B   He varies his schedule according to the group.

    C   He forces everyone to be quick about it.

PAPER 5   SPEAKING (14 minutes)

You take the Speaking test with another candidate, referred to here as your partner. There are two examiners. One will speak to you and your partner and the other will be listening. Both examiners will award marks.

Part 1 (3 minutes)

The examiner asks you and your partner questions about yourselves. You may be asked about things like 'your home town', 'your interests', 'your career plans', etc.

Part 2 (a one-minute 'long turn' for each candidate, plus 20-second response from the second candidate)

The examiner gives you two photographs and asks you to talk about them for one minute. The examiner then asks your partner a question about your photographs and your partner responds briefly.

Then the examiner gives your partner two different photographs. Your partner talks about these photographs for one minute. This time the examiner asks you a question about your partner's photographs and you respond briefly.

Part 3 (approximately 3 minutes)

The examiner asks you and your partner to talk together. You may be asked to solve a problem or try to come to a decision about something. For example, you might be asked to decide the best way to use some rooms in a language school. The examiner gives you a picture to help you but does not join in the conversation.

Part 4 (approximately 4 minutes)

The interlocutor asks some further questions, which leads to a more general discussion of what you have talked about in Part 3. You may comment on your partner's answers if you wish.

UNIVERSITY *of* CAMBRIDGE
ESOL Examinations

SAMPLE

Candidate Name
If not already printed, write name
in CAPITALS and complete the
Candidate No. grid (in pencil).

Candidate Signature

Examination Title

Centre

Supervisor:
If the candidate is ABSENT or has WITHDRAWN shade here ▭

Centre No.

Candidate No.

**Examination
Details**

0	0	0	0
1	1	1	1
2	2	2	2
3	3	3	3
4	4	4	4
5	5	5	5
6	6	6	6
7	7	7	7
8	8	8	8
9	9	9	9

Candidate Answer Sheet

Instructions

Use a PENCIL (B or HB).

Mark ONE letter for each
question.

For example, if you think
B is the right answer to
the question, mark your
answer sheet like this:

0   A B C D E F G H

Rub out any answer you
wish to change using an
eraser.

1	A B C D E F G H
2	A B C D E F G H
3	A B C D E F G H
4	A B C D E F G H
5	A B C D E F G H
6	A B C D E F G H
7	A B C D E F G H
8	A B C D E F G H
9	A B C D E F G H
10	A B C D E F G H
11	A B C D E F G H
12	A B C D E F G H
13	A B C D E F G H
14	A B C D E F G H
15	A B C D E F G H
16	A B C D E F G H
17	A B C D E F G H
18	A B C D E F G H
19	A B C D E F G H
20	A B C D E F G H

21	A B C D E F G H
22	A B C D E F G H
23	A B C D E F G H
24	A B C D E F G H
25	A B C D E F G H
26	A B C D E F G H
27	A B C D E F G H
28	A B C D E F G H
29	A B C D E F G H
30	A B C D E F G H
31	A B C D E F G H
32	A B C D E F G H
33	A B C D E F G H
34	A B C D E F G H
35	A B C D E F G H
36	A B C D E F G H
37	A B C D E F G H
38	A B C D E F G H
39	A B C D E F G H
40	A B C D E F G H

© UCLES 2008   Photocopiable

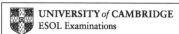

UNIVERSITY *of* CAMBRIDGE
ESOL Examinations

S A M P L E

Candidate Name
If not already printed, write name
in CAPITALS and complete the
Candidate No. grid (in pencil).

Candidate Signature

Examination Title

Centre

Supervisor:
If the candidate is ABSENT or has WITHDRAWN shade here ⊂⊃

Centre No.

Candidate No.

Examination Details

Candidate Answer Sheet

Instructions
Use a PENCIL (B or HB). Rub out any answer you wish to change using an eraser.

Part 1: Mark ONE letter for each question.

For example, if you think **B** is the right
answer to the question, mark your
answer sheet like this:

Parts 2, 3 and **4:** Write your answer clearly
in CAPITAL LETTERS.

For Parts 2 and 3 write one letter
in each box. For example:

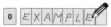

Part 1	Part 2	Do not write below here

Continues over ➡

© UCLES 2008 Photocopiable

© UCLES 2008 Photocopiable

UNIVERSITY *of* **CAMBRIDGE**
ESOL Examinations

SAMPLE

Candidate Name
If not already printed, write name
in CAPITALS and complete the
Candidate No. grid (in pencil).

Candidate Signature

Examination Title

Centre

Supervisor:
If the candidate is ABSENT or has WITHDRAWN shade here ▭

Test version: A B C D E F J K L M N   Special arrangements: S H

Centre No.

Candidate No.

**Examination
Details**

0	0	0	0
1	1	1	1
2	2	2	2
3	3	3	3
4	4	4	4
5	5	5	5
6	6	6	6
7	7	7	7
8	8	8	8
9	9	9	9

Candidate Answer Sheet

Instructions

Use a PENCIL (B or HB).
Rub out any answer you wish to change using an eraser.

Parts 1, 3 and **4:**
Mark ONE letter for each question.

For example, if you think **B** is the
right answer to the question, mark
your answer sheet like this:

Part 2:
Write your answer clearly in CAPITAL LETTERS.

Write one letter or number in each box.
If the answer has more than one word, leave one
box empty between words.

For example:

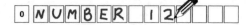

Turn this sheet over to start.

© UCLES 2008   Photocopiable

Part 1

1	A	B	C
2	A	B	C
3	A	B	C
4	A	B	C
5	A	B	C
6	A	B	C
7	A	B	C
8	A	B	C

Part 2 (Remember to write in CAPITAL LETTERS or numbers)

Do not write below here

9		9 1 0 u
10		10 1 0 u
11		11 1 0 u
12		12 1 0 u
13		13 1 0 u
14		14 1 0 u
15		15 1 0 u
16		16 1 0 u
17		17 1 0 u
18		18 1 0 u

Part 3

19	A	B	C	D	E	F
20	A	B	C	D	E	F
21	A	B	C	D	E	F
22	A	B	C	D	E	F
23	A	B	C	D	E	F

Part 4

24	A	B	C
25	A	B	C
26	A	B	C
27	A	B	C
28	A	B	C
29	A	B	C
30	A	B	C

© UCLES 2008 Photocopiable